GOODBYE BADSELL

ADAM PRESTON

Published in 2024 by Particular Media

www.particularmedia.com

Copyright © 2024 by Adam Preston

All rights reserved.

No part of this book may be reproduced in any form or by any electronic or mechanical means, including information storage and retrieval systems, without written permission from the author, except for the use of brief quotations in a book review.

Cover design by Bookconsilio

www.bookconsilio.com

Main cover image from a painting by Celia Preston which, for many years, decorated the Badsell Park Farm leaflet

This book is dedicated to my parents, Simon and Celia Preston

ACKNOWLEDGMENTS

My sincere thanks go to Elizabeth Kirkor Rogers for supporting the creation of this book.

Thanks also to all those who took the time to tell me their Badsell memories. These include my father Simon Preston, my siblings Rupert, Emma, John and Charles Preston, as well as Mark Lucas, Andy Browning, Jose Dadswell, Brian Wiseman, Kenny Wiseman, Nigel Hodges, Ivan Rumary and Gail , Nick and Georgie Belton. Thanks also to the Rogers boys, John, Roland and Andy, in helping to ensure that I received their mother's wonderful photographs of Badsell, many of which are included.

'The Badsell Oak' by Mark Welland, reproduced with the kind permission of the artist

The past is a foreign country: they have no respect for health and safety there.

With apologies to L.P. Hartley

INTRODUCTION

An oak tree once stood in magnificent isolation at Badsell Park Farm towards the edge of the Park Field.

It oversaw my childhood and young adulthood. I climbed it, buried treasure under it, and sat dreaming by it. After my sister's wedding my family lunched under it on tables and chairs transported in the trailer of the Honda three-wheeler motorbike which, at one time or another, nearly killed each one of us.

The oak was so striking that a local fine art photographer, Mark Welland, was inspired to base a substantial part of his oeuvre on the tree, which he named The Badsell Oak. It survived many storms, including the great storm of 1987, but on the night of 27 March 2016 it was felled by Storm Katie.

I no longer lived on the farm but local farmer, Adam Wise, kindly transported two of its limbs, balancing them on the front forks of a tractor, all the way to my home near Castle Hill about four miles away.

I planned to make a commemorative chopping board but the logs started to rot. Occasionally it occurred to me that the 'Badsell years' were quickly receding.

INTRODUCTION

Lunch beneath the Badsell Oak the day after
Emma's wedding

From the mid 1960s through to the late 1990s, Badsell Park Farm was an arable farm, as it is now, but it was also a rare breeds park or petting zoo, a fruit and vegetable farm, and a pick-your-own farm with a farm shop. It had a café and a gift shop and a nature trail.

You could take a tractor and trailer ride or, if you preferred, a carriage ride, courtesy of a heavy horse called Lady Eleanor. There were riding stables and pony and donkey rides, a butterfly house and Trinidadian leaf cutter ant house. For a while there was a large purpose-built mouse mansion complete with mouse portraits on the walls and a kitchen fire over which a fake leg of lamb was turned by a mouse wheel. There were pigs that lived at Badsell whose pictures still decorate people's homes thirty years on. There were events ranging from dog shows and pet shows to Guy Fawkes Nights. From an Andean Festival, at which the ambassadors of various South American nations nearly came to blows, to a Cowboy-themed barn dance during which a barroom brawl was staged with real stunt men. It was a place where people didn't just live and work, but where people from different backgrounds were thrown together to form a loose community and almost overwhelmingly happy memories.

One day I found a message on my answer machine from an old family friend called Elizabeth Kirkor Rogers. Known to us as 'Lizzie' she was a close friend of my mother's. She now lives in New York.

"Adam I'm going to commission you," she said. "I want you to write a book about Badsell Park Farm. I don't want all those stories to be lost."

Goodbye Badsell is a very personal account of those Badsell years. I should apologise for placing myself so much at the heart of the story, but that is the perspective from which I experienced things. I have also reached out to people for whom Badsell was a special place and many have generously given me their time to tell me their stories. What has struck me is just how important 'the farm' was to people. More than one described their years at Badsell as the best and happiest of their lives. There are many more people who will feel that they too should have been asked to contribute but I have had to draw the line somewhere.

My hope is that *Goodbye Badsell* captures the spirit of Badsell Park Farm during a specific time in a way that a chopping board never could. It is an eccentric book — a hodgepodge of personal memories, family history, anecdotes, descriptions of people, places and events, thrown together in an occasionally not entirely logical manner. It probably would have made sense to put all the near-fatal accidents caused by the Honda three-wheeler into one chapter. My hope is that the book is a bit like Badsell itself was in those years — chaotic but charming.

I have included a lot of images in the book which are black and white in this edition, but most can be seen in colour in the e

INTRODUCTION

book and I will make a colour print version available which, unfortunately, will be expensive due to the added printing costs.

I have tried to give credit to the photographers where I can but I would like to thank everyone who has sent photographs and any errors in the captions will be put right in subsequent editions. If you spot any mistakes in the book or wish to add something please contact me at adamprestonauthor@gmail.com and I will try to make the appropriate amendments in subsequent editions.

CHAPTER 1
INTERLOPERS

It all began when an old London dock worker electrocuted his balls.

In the 1960s my parents came into some money and they started to think about buying a farm. My Mum, Celia, was the real driving force behind this — she wanted to be a farmer but perhaps most of all she wanted to be immersed in country life.

After they married, my parents bought Fowle Hall near Laddingford in Kent, but after living there a while a problem emerged.

The previous owner had suffered financial losses which forced him to sell the house to my parents. He and his wife also suffered the heartbreaking loss of their little boy. They moved into a smaller property next door.

When my sister Emma was born in the house in 1965 the situation became untenable. The farmer's wife simply could not hide her bitterness. It cannot have been easy for her to see my parents, who were rather a glamorous young couple with their growing family, in what she probably regarded as 'her' house.

Simon and Celia on their wedding day, 1964

After a short time my parents realised that they could not go on living there and they sold up and moved away. It is perhaps worth mentioning that later the farmer and his wife had a daughter and she visited my parents at Badsell, so in the end there were no hard feelings.

While they lived at Fowle Hall, my parents became very friendly with their chatty and characterful 'daily woman,' Emmie Marsh. Emmie's husband, Ted Marsh, was a farm labourer who worked on a farm on Crittenden Lane near Matfield.

Next my parents rented quite a grand house called Court Lodge in Chelsfield but they had by this point decided to try and find a farm and they started viewing farms in roughly a fifteen mile radius around Paddock Wood railway station, so that Dad could commute to London.

As they started to look at farms, Mum and Dad would some-

CHAPTER 1

times take Ted along with them, figuring he would be a good person to offer practical advice. My parents had also become friendly with Emmie's younger sister, Kath, who was married to Ernie Wiseman, a London dustman. If it was the weekend then, when they went to view farms, Ernie would come too.

My father is what, in the old days, would be called a 'gent'. His grandfather was a multi-millionaire called Sir Frederick Preston and he is the great great great great nephew of Britain's greatest naval hero, Horatio Nelson.

Celia and Simon with their first child, Rupert, at Fowle Hall, 1964

For a while Dad wore a pin-striped suit and stiff collar to his job as the first ever public relations officer at the Stock Exchange in the City of London. He was just 25 and used to show people like The Duke of Windsor around, and entertain people in the executive private restaurant where extra fat cigarettes were handed out free from a silver box . When Lizzie Rogers visited my parents at their flat in London, before they moved to Fowle Hall, Lizzie's mother was shocked to find towels embroidered with the names 'Simon' and 'Valerie' in the bathroom. She didn't realise that 'Valerie' was his yacht and assumed he was brazenly dating multiple women.

By the time of his first trip to Badsell Park Farm, Dad was

working at Lazzards, the posh merchant bank, where his job was to make sure that the press never printed anything about Lazzards at all.

Emmie Marsh

On that very first visit to Badsell, Mum and Dad not only took Ted and Ernie, but also Ted and Ernie's father-in-law, Frederick Abdi, a militant left-wing London dock worker. His grandson, Brian, remembers him affectionately as a 'horrible old bugger'.

This unlikely group were having a look around Badsell Park Farm and at one point they all had to climb over an electric fence. Fred Abdi got stuck with one leg over the fence and got a whopping great shock to his bollocks. He hollered in pain and Ted and Ernie, his two sons-in-law, fell about laughing.

I am sure other things happened that day but it is perhaps a useful indicator, at this early stage, that in my family the electrification of a man's balls is the only thing that needed to be recorded for posterity. No other details of that first look around Badsell Park Farm have survived.

Emma and Rupert in a hop garden near Fowle Hall

The farm at that time was owned by a very wealthy landowner called Billings who had land all over the South East of England. He owned a large part of the farmland on the Isle of Wight, some say as much as a third of it.

He had a farm labourer called Frost who was practically camping in the semi-derelict farmhouse at Badsell. In my father's words Frost was "almost a peasant". By day Frost was doing the basic things required to keep the place going while pretty much every inch of the land was under barley. For the ploughing, sowing, harvesting and other work on the fields, Billings would send men and machinery from his other farms. There was an apple orchard behind the house but the trees were mature and it required huge wooden ladders to get up into the branches to do the pruning and picking.

Billings was a tough man to negotiate with. Mum and Dad went to Dartford to thrash out the deal and when my father asked him why he was selling the land he made out that Badsell was an inconvenient outlying property which he wanted to sell in order to streamline his operation. In retrospect my father thinks he overpaid for the place because of the poor quality of the soil. But Mum had fallen for Badsell and they paid the asking price which was £80k.

Kath and Ernie Wiseman at the Kent Arms near Fowle Hall, 1960. Photo: Kenny Wiseman

My parents bought Badsell Park Farm in 1966, a few months after I was born, and they moved there shortly after my Christening which took place on the day England won the World Cup against Germany at Wembley.

Once they had purchased the farm one of the first things my parents did was to hire Ted as their farm labourer and he moved into one of the two cottages opposite the farmhouse.

Before this Dad went to visit Ted's then employer, Ben Thomsett, on Crittenden Lane, a courtesy call to inform him that he would be employing Ted.

Thompsett was not pleased.

He inferred that my father was an 'interloper' from London and that this poaching of labourers was not 'the done thing'. He

CHAPTER 1

then rounded off the conversation by adding, "He's no bloody good anyway!"

Thompsett didn't speak to my parents for ten years after that - but once the ten years were up they became quite friendly.

Celia with John Rogers, 1966 (collection of Elizabeth Kirkor Rogers)

Ted Marsh at Badsell

CHAPTER 2
BOG HOLE

What my parents purchased in 1966 was 185 acres of poor quality Kentish clay soil in a gentle valley, broken up into nine fields with various patches of woodland. On the earliest Ordinance Survey map (circa 1805) the property is referred to as Bog Hole.

Rupert in front of the farmhouse prior to the
extension built in 1972

When my parents took over there was the semi derelict

CHAPTER 2

farmhouse where Frost had been living his peasant existence, the attached pair of cottages opposite, and various farm buildings, the main ones clustered around a farmyard.

The farm was reached, and still is today, by coming off the main Tunbridge Wells to Maidstone Road (the A228) onto the narrow meandering Crittenden Lane which makes its way eventually to the village of Matfield. In summer the road is a tunnel of green, as the hazel, oak, chestnut and other trees meet above you. A similar tunnel of green is encountered coming the other way, down the hill from Matfield. Either way you dive into a deep emerald otherworld before reaching the driveway at the bottom of the valley as it crosses the Tudely Brook.

The drive is straight and just under a quarter of a mile long, with a little rise a short way in. The drive eventually leads you into the farmyard then continues onwards into the valley, in the early days as a dirt track used only by farm vehicles.

At the time of buying it, the farmhouse was not particularly impressive in appearance but the heart of it was over 250 years old. The downstairs room has an immense fireplace and the beam over it bears an inscription stating 'The R.H HON.ABL THE EARLE OF WESTMORELAND FTK 1712.'

This room is believed to have been a hunting lodge on the estate of the Earl. When Rupert was a little boy he wrote a letter to the then current Earl, quoting the inscription. We anticipated an invitation to a huge castle and a massive feast to celebrate this exciting connection. Instead Rupert received a terse reply. I have since worked out that the TFK stands for Thomas Fane Knight, thanks to Maximilian Fane, a descendant. Thomas Fane was the 6th Earl of Westmoreland and he owned Badsell Manor, though he preferred to live at Mereworth Castle.

The 'hunting lodge' forms the old heart of the farmhouse. To the left of the fireplace is a stairway which, when we lived there, was hidden behind a secret door covered with a bookshelf. The stairway leads up to a low ceilinged 'master bedroom' with wide plank floors polished a deep mahogany. This room was our parent's bedroom in our early childhood, but was later taken over by my sister Emma and then later still by John and Charles, 'The Twins'.

After living in the farmhouse for a few years my parents extended it, the work beginning in 1972. The night before the work was to start, they happened to have an architect friend come to the house for dinner. He took one look at the plans and insisted they stop the work immediately as the plans were simply wrong. The correct thing to do was to repeat the shape of the left side of the house on the right, creating a smart manor house. Mum could see that he was right but Dad was just infuriated at the delay and they had a huge row, after which it was agreed to follow the architect's advice.

This extension added considerably to the size of the house and Rupert and I moved up into a vast open area on the third floor, reached by a vertiginously steep old narrow staircase that had once lead to a couple of attic rooms. At first we shared this space but later Rupert persuaded my parents to build him a couple of walls and a door, creating a private bedroom. My room became everything around it. I had a built-in wardrobe on which I painted a portrait of George Orwell and it is a very obscure fact that Orwell's father was a descendent of the 8th Earl of Westmoreland.

Up in these attic rooms Rupert and I had storage heaters filled with bricks which came on at night when electricity was cheap. They had glass tops and I almost immediately shattered mine when I sat on it while attempting to warm myself. The storage heaters meant that in freezing mid winter these top rooms were the warmest in the house in the morning - just when you had to get up and leave. I thought I had solved this problem when Mum gave us long thermal underwear to keep warm

CHAPTER 2

during a particularly freezing winter. I draped mine over the storage heater but when I reached across to put them on in the morning the pants had melted.

Coming up the drive of Badsell the first building you encounter is a long open-fronted hay barn on your right, with a closed shed attached. During my early childhood this shed was always locked and contained a vast Rolls Royce under a canvas cover. We kids could squeeze into the shed, despite the lock, and inside was a place of almost total darkness. We would then find our way inside the Rolls Royce itself which, because it was completely covered with a fitted tarpaulin, was even darker. Inside one could sense, rather than see, the immense quality of a vintage Rolls Royce interior. Years later I learned that the car belonged to Neil North, the actor who played the boy in the 1948 film version of 'The Winslow Boy.' He was the brother of Desmond North, a friend of my parents who lived in East Peckham.

The farmhouse and farmyard from the air

After the hay barn the pair of attached cottages were also on the right shortly afterwards. After they purchased the farm my parents moved into one of these while the farmhouse was being renovated and Ted moved into the other. Later Ernie Wiseman and his wife Kath would move into the second of the two, and here they would raise their two boys, Brian, and Steve, and their eldest Kenny would continue his working life. My grandmother, Ruth, lived for a while in the first cottage and from 1976 her son Nick would come and stay mid week, commuting to his office in Blackfriars.

When we first moved to Badsell there were also substantial hopper huts across the field from the hay barn, behind the two cottages, in what became The Horse Field, though they were rotting and falling apart. These hopper huts had housed seasonal hop pickers, often from the East End of London, who picked hops as a holiday activity. Kath and Ernie had been amongst them, although they never picked at Badsell.

As kids we spent many hours playing amongst the dilapidated remains of these hopper huts which had been slightly raised off the ground, so that there were dark cavernous spaces beneath the rotting floor boards which we would crawl into and play amidst the dried earth.

Later, in the farm shop, we installed a diorama commemorating the hop picking heritage of the farm. It showed a man and a woman picking hops and featured a pair of old shop manakins. The whole thing was suspended above the till in the gift shop. When we were creating the scene, my friend Johnny Drake, who had a bit if a reputation for clumsiness, dropped the man's head, sheering off the paint on one side of his face. To disguise this, his head had to be forever turned sharply away from the public, as though he was afraid of being recognised. Johnny got over his clumsiness and is now a successful building engineer putting up skyscrapers in Australia.

After passing the two cottages the drive took you into the farmyard which consisted, on the right, of an extremely long single story wooden building painted in black pitch.

The first part of this was a large wooden shed, followed by a beautiful brick and wood stable block, the floors of which were covered with immense smooth rounded cobbles. Inside were

CHAPTER 2

three solidly built stables, the last of which allowed the horses to look out into the yard.

Beyond the stables was a small room which was always known as 'The Poison Shed'. It smelled exactly as a poison shed should - a sinister invasive stink that you felt was killing you by the minute. It had a heavy padlock and the key hung on an upright beam nearby. When, as kids, we wanted to enter the Poison Shed we simply took down the key and unlocked it. I used to hold my breath when I was in there.

The yard showing the Long Barn during the Badsell Park Fayre, 1992

After this the building continued with an open fronted sheltered area where, at seven in the morning, Mum would meet Ernie Wiseman to discuss the day's work for roughly the next twenty years.

After this, the same long building continued with another shed (which later became the public toilet) and beyond that a tar pit where the hop poles had once been dipped.

Coming into the farmyard on your left was a double oast house.

Badsell Park Farm is in Kent and Kent, during the heyday of English hop growing, was by far the biggest hop growing county. At Badsell there is a classic roundel and a large oblong double oast of more modern design, topped by a pair of louvred oblong wooden housings containing electric fans to draw the heat and smoke up through the hops that were laid out on the slats in two large 'reeks' below. One of these housings became our secret den, unreachable by adults. The two big fans were still working right through until the place was converted into a house at the end of the 20th Century, some years after my family had left.

Simon, Emma and John and Charles Preston in front of the 'poison shed' by the stables

The height of hop growing in England was the later part of the 19th Century when 72,000 acres of hop gardens existed in the country, almost three quarters of them in Kent. The decline began in the 1890's when the government began to tax beer and the death knell was rung by hop wilt and cheap imports in the 1950s. Kent hop growing had been in steep decline for decades by the time my parents bought the place in 1966, and hop gardens were rapidly being grubbed out all over Kent.

There was a lot of evidence of the previous use of the land at Badsell for hop growing but the farm's hop gardens had been grubbed out by the time we arrived. Our friends Rupert and Pat Hodges, however, still had seventy five acres under

CHAPTER 2

hops at Tattingbury Farm near Five Oak Green where they had six roundels. They farmed hops up until around 1988/89. Their son Nigel came back from a trip to Australia before this and he took over from George Simmonds on the farm. He recalls that, during his time, the hops were dried using diesel burners in the kilns with the hops laid out on sacking to a depth of three feet in the 'reeks' above. Judging how much moisture the hops contained was crucial and dictated how long they had to be dried (anything between five and nine hours). At the height of the picking season in September, they were bagging up to thirty 'pockets' of hops a day but price fluctuations meant that it was a high risk crop. One year they did so well Rupert took his family on a three week holiday to Kenya, which included an extended safari on the Maasai Mara, but at the end the price dropped so low they made nothing at all.

The roundel at Badsell, when we arrived, was still full of black ash from the last fires that had been lit in the kiln. As a small child, when the doors were closed, this would have been the darkest place I knew in the universe, had it not been for the Rolls Royce halfway up the drive.

At the side of the 'modern' oast house was 'the gantry' a huge wooden balcony, with a corrugated iron roof and sides. This is where the green hops had been stored before being laid out on the slatted drying floors above the two big oblong kilns. The gantry housed a diesel tank which was used for tractor fuel.

Beneath the gantry was a rough steep slope of bare dry earth where I spent many hours playing as a small child. One of my earliest memories is of a very heavy downpour of rain which caused rivulets to run down this slope into the wide open drain at the bottom. Because of the corrugated iron roof the sound of the rain was deafening. Combined with thunder and lightning the whole thing was incredibly dramatic. I became a great manufacturer of mud - converting the dry dust to mud in various containers for hours on end in a state of bliss.

After being dried the hops were moved to the upstairs cooling floor in the central part of the oast house, known as the stowage. When they were ready to be packed the hops were scuppetted into hop pockets through a hole in the centre of the floor (covered over and used by us as a rollerskating jump).

Next to the gantry was a large Atcost barn, a concrete reinforced building with an asbestos roof. It had huge double wooden sliding doors at both ends and would be used for all kinds of things over the years, including a 'most alike' twin contest, a circus performance, my sister's wedding banquet and many illegal raves in the 1990s. Of course it was also used to store apples, grain, rapeseed, and other agricultural produce. When my parents bought the farm it came with a vast number of wooden apple boxes which we used to store apples and pears but which were gradually diminished. If a single panel was broken a box was instantly condemned and smashed up for firewood. These boxes now change hands for large sums of money.

Emma at her wedding banquet in the big barn

CHAPTER 2

For several years the Atcost barn contained a baby grand piano that my brother Rupert gave to my sister on her wedding day. He got it for free but he had to collect it. He called all his friends and offered them a pint and we heaved it out of a basement window and up a steep slope, over some metal railings and into a van before it was driven to Badsell.

After a few years of running the petting zoo my parents converted the barn into a proper 'play barn' providing a much needed wet-weather option for parents. Up until then, if it was raining, pretty much nobody came to the farm. The building was clad, and insulated, given a proper door and entranceway on the side and a minstrels gallery with a slide that took you back down to the floor of the huge main room. The piano had by then become horribly abused by children and eventually it was condemned.

Adam at work on the giant pig painting that would decorate the playbarn

Of course they had to get planning permission for all this work as this was officially 'change of use'. My mother had a deep fear of the kind of petty officials involved in this process and when a woman from Tunbridge Wells Borough Council came to look at the site she indicated that she was 'mindful to approve' the work but hoped that we did not intend to apply for permission to hold wedding celebrations. She only said this because she had been involved with a rash of applications for wedding licences and she was bored of them - but Mum took it to heart and never applied. This is one of the great 'what ifs', because Badsell would have made an exceptional wedding venue.

To decorate the play barn, I created a life-sized painting of 'the largest pig that ever lived.' I had found a print of this animal, standing with its top-hatted handler, in *The Ark,* a magazine about rare breeds which Mum subscribed to. I calculated how big it would have been in real life and painted a massive canvas, using the minstrels gallery of the play barn as a studio. The painting hung in the barn for years. Eventually I sold it to nearby Groombridge Place and its current whereabouts are unknown.

There were two more significant buildings on the farm. Next to the gantry was quite a substantial barn which my parents demolished — something they regretted later. A lot of buildings were taken down in the countryside in the 1960s — including substantial country houses. This was long before the property boom when every farm building was turned onto a house.

Barn in the farmhouse garden that was demolished

Another substantial structure was an open-fronted building

we called the 'bullock barn' which was also painted with black pitch and had fine upright timbers supporting the front, on stone bases. There were also fine built-in wooden mangers and later we created animal pens around them. Adjoining the bullock barn was a decent sized corrugated tin shed which became 'the pet shed'. Near the bullock barn was another open fronted corrugated iron-roofed building which was used as a second straw and hay store and later as the 'chicken display' (and later still, in part, the butterfly house).

The two largest fields at Badsell were the Park Field (host to The Badsell Oak) and the Sloping Field. The Little Orchard was either side of the drive and The Horse Field lay behind the two cottages. There was a long area that began behind the stables that was never named but included The Pear Orchard. Beyond this was The End Field. On the left side of the dirt track that lead down the valley was The Blackberries, followed by The Sewer Field which was reached by crossing a small bridge then following a track that had tributaries of The Tudely Brook and woodland running either side of it.

Emma by the oast. An apple box made a useful cup stand. (Circa 1979, Photo: Kevin Walsh)

CHAPTER 3
THE TUDELY BROOK

Badsell Park Farm was a paradise for children. The farmhouse is far from any road, there are woods, fields, barns, a million places to build camps and a little meandering steam called the Tudely Brook.

My mother had experienced her own version of a childhood paradise when the Thornely family left India in 1944 while the Second World War was still raging - travelling on the ship RMS Otranto. It was considered dangerous to live near London so her father, Frank Thornely, rented a house called Broomclose near Porlock in Somerset for his wife Ruth, two boys, Nick and Anto, and daughter Celia.

They shared the house with lots of cousins but with the men all away it was a gathering of mothers with children. It included Mary McLeod (Frank's sister) and her boys Donald and Ian, Winifred Barnes and her children Jill and Tim, and Sheila Barker (Ruth's older sister) and her children Anne, Rosemary and Peter.

Rationing was still on but it was a beautiful rural setting, close to the coast, and the children ran wild. They rode their bicycles to Porlock Wier or to the pebbly beach near Minehead

CHAPTER 3

and there was a pony. My mother recalled that the women, all products of the 'Raj', were accustomed to having servants, and were having to get to grips with domestic chores for the first time. Winifred found the washing up particularly taxing and would step away halfway through and announce, "I'll just leave that there."

My early memories of Badsell are hard to date because I lived there from the age of six months. I have a very early memory of standing outside the back door, where the Tudely Brook comes close to the back door of the farmhouse.

There was a low brick wall running along by the stream, with a big drop down to the water. The wall teemed with tiny red spiders, possibly the whirligig mite. The back door area faced south and was a sun trap where Mum hung out the washing.

Celia, Nick and Anto Thornely

A little later I recall being out in the yard and finding a can of fuel, probably paraffin, in the first shed on the right after the two cottages. It was a workshop that was very badly lit and full of old farm tools. I was mucking about and I poured paraffin over my hand. A man, I have no idea who he was, came across me and told me my hand was going to burst into flames at any moment. Terrified I ran back to the farmhouse.

During those early years I was the classic 'freckle faced kid' and always seemed to be wearing a T-shirt with a picture of Charlie Brown bearing the legend "I need all the friends I can get." Grown ups found the T-shirt funny but I didn't really understand it.

One of the constants in my childhood were nettle stings. Wearing wellies and shorts I would make my way down to the Tudely Brook for a paddle and would step gingerly through nettles thinking I could avoid them like a ninja. Suddenly I would feel the shocking pain and feel an overwhelming sense of injustice. We learned early to rub dock leaves on the sting and would sometimes rub and rub until the whole area was stained green. I have since learned that dock does no good at all but there was a placebo affect.

If we were feeling brave we would paddle under the low bridge by the farmhouse, where our voices bounced off the low ceiling. The water is a bit deeper here and the chances of water suddenly gushing in and filling your wellies was ever-present. Under stones and at the edges, beneath overhanging ridges, lurked stone loaches and common bullheads.

I learned to lift a rock with immense care and stealth. Any fish beneath did not necessarily dart away, but sometimes remained on the bottom in full sight, swaying gently in the current.

I would then dip a transparent plastic bag into the water and draw its open mouth towards the back end of the fish, so that the bottom part of the bag was stretched across the stream bottom, just above the ground. I could then slowly envelop the unknowing fish and catch it.

CHAPTER 3

Adam and Emma playing in the Tudely Brook near the back door of the farmhouse in the early 1970s

When paddling about in the stream the moment would come when you would step out of your depth and freezing water rushed into your wellies. Because the stream was largely shaded it never warmed up, even in summer, and it was bone-achingly cold. But only occasionally would I choose to abandon the expedition. So immersed would I be in what I was doing that I would carry on, with the water sloshing about and eventually being warmed by my body heat.

Often we would climb into the stream at an accessible point and then just head upstream and see how far we could go. The Tudely Brook would alternate between wide shallows, with tiny gravelly beaches at the bends, with deeps which, particularly when younger, would defeat us and cause us to head home. Occasionally you would come across a pool with whirligig beetles at rest on the surface and they would begin swimming madly in circles when they saw you. They were very hard to catch, being incredibly quick and capable of diving, but just occasionally I would get one and stare in wonder at this cheeky little black jewel before releasing it.

These deeps were often caused by natural damns caused by

fallen trees or logs and other detritus that had been shifted during a heavy winter downpour, but a common game was to build a damn with rocks and this would become utterly engrossing. You would hunt bigger and bigger stones and start to feel like you really could conquerer nature and stop the flow of the river. One afternoon I spent many hours with my cousin Sam at a section of the stream at the end of The Blackberry Field. There was one part which ran faster and this we christened 'The Roaring Forties". Inevitably another part of the stream was "The Bermuda Triangle", a particular obsession with small boys in the 1970's.

After these trips I would return to the house, my boots making a squelching sound, and I would empty them out on the back doorstep. By this point my socks had always worked their way down to my toes.

As the third born child I was the baby of the family, or at least I was for nine years.

As the baby I watched my older brother and sister with awe. They were always ahead of me, doing more advanced things, and I was constantly frustrated that they were stronger, faster and cleverer. My brother was so much stronger that he could, on a whim, pin me to the ground and sit on my face, then release a fart. He called this 'cauliflower time'.

Just occasionally my older siblings would have an argument and it would escalate and explode into violence. For me this was like seeing King Kong versus Godzilla - it would feel like my whole world was being torn apart. I adored them both and the idea of them turning on each other terrified me.

The one thing that drove me into an instant rage was if someone called me a 'baby' and Rupert quickly caught on to this. He would sing the words *"Adam's a baby"* to the tune of *"Bring out the Branston"* from a TV advertisement for Branston Pickle. This (ironically) would make me cry like a baby. Mum was always trying to explain to me that I only had to stop reacting to Rupert's teasing and the torment would stop.

Rupert, Emma and Adam at the front door of the farmhouse, circa 1968

Despite the fact that Rupert was an absolute devil I idolised him. He was a mischievous monkey, always pushing the boundaries, breaking every rule and getting away with every outrage on account of being funny and cute. He made fun of everyone around him and had endless absurd names for Dad such as 'Rigid' and 'Dune', the origins of which were obscure even then.

Before one of his birthdays, Rupert informed my parents that he wanted an Action Man as his present. My father found himself in Harrods and, not being one of nature's shoppers, he grabbed something that struck him as being very close to an Action Man, even if it was actually called 'Little Big Man'. When Rupert opened the gift he was underwhelmed by Little Big Man's macho credentials but was delighted at the hilarity of Dad buying such an unimpressive soldier. To emphasise the point he took off its uniform and reclothed it in clothes from

Emma's dolls, then rechristened him 'The Fairy of the Front Line'. The toy took its place amongst Rupert's favourites. Amongst these were a collection of rubber dogs known as the 'Dog Mob' who were always on their way somewhere. You would come across them half way down the attic stairs or making their way along the upstairs corridor, frozen in the act of travel.

When a hamster died Rupert replaced the animal with some rubber gorillas which gave Nan (our grandmother Ruth Thornely) a shock when she peered through the bars one day to see what was living in there. In Rupert's memory the gorillas had 'anatomically correct genitals.'

For a while my favourite toy was a teddy bear that Mum had sewn a special outfit for. She was a trained seamstress and she worked from a design which had caught my eye in a book. It was painstaking work but she did it beautifully and I was thrilled with the result. A little later I became very attached to a tiny cheap dun-coloured Chinese-made teddy bear. He was my best friend, confidant and hero, somewhere between Jesus and Superman. He lead a hodgepodge of other toys, steering them through every war and crisis and solving problems with deep wisdom and compassion. My relationship with Little Ted became even more important when I was sent away to boarding school aged eight. Small for my age, a late developer and a dreamy kid with my head in the clouds, boarding school was a bewildering experience made bearable by the constant presence of Little Ted in my grey corduroy shorts' pocket.

At some point he went missing and I was inconsolable. My mother was contacted and she drove in specially with a replacement. It was winter and I met her in the main hallway of the school on a dark evening. She handed over a long limbed bright yellow bear that bore no relationship to my little soul mate and I

CHAPTER 3

was crushed. I was racked with guilt anyway, at putting my mother to such inconvenience.

(Left to right) Adam, Emma and Rupert, circa 1969

Many years later, in my twenties, Little Teds began to appear at Badsell.

One was hidden behind the shutters in the room to the left of the front door of the farmhouse. Another was found in the guttering of the big oast. Other appeared in attic niches and other clever hiding places.

This was more than a decade after the bears had gone missing but Rupert owned up to having hidden them all. Behind the scenes, my poor mother had been striving to replace the bear each time my older brother had hidden him.

I did not often get the better of my older brother but an opportunity came in the 1970s when we held a mini Olympic games at Badsell for all our friends. We had a multitude of events including a wheelbarrow race, apple bobbing, something we called 'bicycle bending' (a slalom race), and welly throwing. Because this was the 1970s there was no consideration for anyone being smaller or younger and there were no 'participation medals'. It was Darwinian survival of the biggest, strongest, fastest, and fittest.

The big event was the cross country run which began with

us running across the bridge by the farmhouse and took us up into the Park Field. We ran to the top and then through the wood into the sloping field, then down to cross the stream and back along the valley into the yard.

There were about thirty kids running but because we actually lived there my brother and I obviously had the advantage. We knew the terrain. But I had no advantage over my brother who was a good three years older.

Yet somehow, as we came down the home stretch towards the yard, I had a small lead. Rupert was behind me and he was determined to beat me — the thought of being outrun by his younger brother was unbearable.

But I smelled glorious victory and, digging deep, I managed to hold that lead as I passed the big barn and approached the finish line by the stables.

Even better my Uncle, Nick Thornely, was there with his super-8 camera to record the moment, capturing for all time both Rupert's agony and my exhausted ecstasy.

Needless to say, this being the 1970s, and despite this remarkable achievement, my aggregated points from the other events did not place me amongst the medalists - but as this is my book I get to finally celebrate this triumph.

We were always building dens at Badsell and one stands out in particular.

It was in a bit of woodland we didn't go to very often, close to Crittenden Lane on the edge of the Park Field. For some reason someone had hoisted a filthy old sack up into the tree beneath which we built the den out of sticks. As a result Rupert christened it "The Hanging Biggie". For us the word 'biggie' meant 'poo' — so this name was absolutely hilarious. Around this time a novelty toy came into our lives which we thought was the best thing in the world. It was called "The Laughing Bag." It was a device in a cotton bag which, when you pressed a button, laughed uproariously for an annoyingly long time. The Hanging Biggie and The Laughing Bag seem to sum up this period of early childhood.

A favourite 'den' was situated high above the two furnaces in the big oast house. On top of the roof were two louvred rectangular housings containing large fans. These two adjoining constructions could be accessed through a trap door but only if you had the courage to climb a precipitous rope ladder hanging above the slatted floor. As you clambered up you had to be careful not to look down or you might glimpse, not just the floor below, but, through the open slatted planks, the floor below that as well. Later the rope ladder was replaced with an immensely long old wooden apple picking ladder which made the climb a little safer but still too off putting for adults.

Adam beating Rupert in the cross country race.
Stills taken from Nick Thornely's super-8 film of the event, circa 1973

The prize though, was worth it, because the little wooden house above was every kid's dream — a place to which no adult dared venture due to the terrifying climb. Rupert quickly caught on to the potential and began dragging things up there. Lamps, drapes, a mattress, a record player. Soon he had a private den of iniquity where he could smoke, drink, invite girls and do everything that you are not meant to do in your teens. He had a pack of saucy playing cards up there too, for playing poker with his friends. The cards were German and therefore deeply kinky, featuring women in elaborate lingerie.

Another item which Rupert took up into the den in the sky was an air rifle which he used to fire at the buttocks of our sister Emma's friends.

There was a second identical little 'den in the sky' adjoining the first one, but this one was even more difficult to access. You had to squeeze your way in from the first one and it involved clambering over the open trap door and the abyss below it. It remained empty and unused — a sanctuary for pigeons.

When we were kids, Rupert, Emma and I occasionally climbed up onto the roof of the farmhouse if Mum and Dad foolishly left us unattended. We would crawl out through the tiny first floor bathroom window and crawl right up onto the roof where we found a whole world of undreamed of spaces and vistas. Occasionally, as we crawled about, one of the old roof tiles would come loose and slide away, smashing on the ground far below.

The farmhouse also has numerous loft spaces that can be reached by various doors and hatches. I loved crawling about in these and visiting the various nests beneath the eaves, usually occupied by families of starlings. I would hand feed the chicks with worms. I once put my foot through the floor and it came out through the ceiling above the main stairway.

CHAPTER 3

Climbing onto the roof. Left to right: Andy Rogers, Emma, Adam, Steven Wiseman, John Rogers, 1971 (collection of Elizabeth Kirkor Rogers)

The upstairs area in the big oast, known as the 'stowage,' had been used before we lived at the farm to cool the hops before they were packed into hop pockets down through another trap door leading to the substantial area below (which later became the huge sprawling gift shop).

This upstairs area was reached by climbing an enormous narrow wooden staircase which was almost as terrifying as the vast ladder leading to the secret den, although it did have a handrail. The large room above became our 'kids domain' in early childhood and a local friend, Jose Dadswell, made some tie dye curtains which were tattered rags by the time we left the farm. The room really came into its own when we were given roller skates one Christmas and we would spend hours going round and round on the wooden floor, occasionally doing little jumps on the trap door cover.

From this area you could also access the smaller slatted floor in the 'reek' of the roundel of the smaller oast house, although we never made much use of this room. Between the slatted floors the small cross beams bore a layer of fine black dust, several inches deep, and if you did anything in there this dust would be dislodged, particularly unwelcome when the roundel below became the farm shop. The reek was only really ever used for a bit of storage and when we started featuring a Santas Grotto below. Then it was used to sprinkle snow.

One great advantage of growing up on a farm away from a road is that you get to drive vehicles. At one point Rupert got his hands on a fully functioning Mini. We painted a massive strawberry on the roof and used it to race around the fields. In the 1970s my father bought one of the first Range Rovers. It was pale blue with plastic ochre seats and a drop down gate at the rear. We would sit on this in a row and took turns to steer, racing across the stubble after the harvest. Rupert also had a motorbike for a while and inevitably he came off and, in one of the more serious accidents that occurred, he knocked a tooth out of a customer's child.

We were, in my opinion, amongst the luckiest kids in the world. We lived within our own land, were free to roam, and to endlessly make our own play and amusement. I did not yearn to go somewhere else, except when the fairground came to Tunbridge Wells by Major York's Road and it occurred to me that I could get there by bicycle. I made the journey one afternoon on the yellow 'racer' that my Mum had bought me from the Cash and Carry.

On arrival I realised that going on fairground rides on your own is no fun at all. I went instead to the amusement arcade and started playing the two penny slot machine where great piles of two pennies were teetering on the edge, poised to avalanche down. Various feral children started to take an interest in my activities and I started to feel like a county bumpkin — a rosy cheeked innocent who had stumbled amongst wolves.

When I caused one of the big teetering stacks of two pence pieces to collapse I reached for my winnings only to find several grubby little hands grabbing my money. I was soon back on my bike heading home, feeling desperate for the safe embrace of Badsell.

CHAPTER 3

So lucky were we that for one summer we even had a swimming pool. It was a 'farmer's pool'. A digger dug the hole, with a deep end and shallow end, and the whole thing was then lined with thick black plastic sheeting, with bare earth beneath it. I recall the agony of waiting outside the back door, on a very hot day, because it was believed to be dangerous for children to swim immediately after lunch.

Rupert on his motorbike with John and Charles

I think my parents had got the idea of making a pool from Rupert Hodges, a local hop farmer, who already had one. On one occasion we went there with Brian and Steven Wiseman, Ernie's kids, and there was a lot of fighting over a huge inflatable black inner tube from a tractor that was the pools only toy. Brian, being the biggest, took possession of this thing and at one point I sank to the bottom of the pool.

I could not swim and I was now drowning. Because of the black lining I had a sense of sinking into a fathomless black abyss.

I was yanked out by Brian who therefore gets the credit for saving my life, even if his hogging of the inner tube had nearly ended it. As for our pool at Badsell - it only lasted one or maybe two summers before, inevitably, it sprung a leak. I felt guilty about this as, on a rainy winter's day, I couldn't resist throwing stones in it and I always wondered if one of them had made a hole in the black plastic. The result was that the pool lost most of its water which soon turned green. It eventually reverted to being a duck pond and it came into its own later, forming part of the pet area.

When we were still quite little Rupert, Emma and I started walking to the village of Matfield to buy sweets. Until then the only time we got to buy anything was when the ice cream van arrived on the farm. It came very seldom and only in the summer months.

We started walking to Matfield when I was as young as four years old and it was a round trip of around three miles. We would walk to the top of the sloping field and enter the woods, walking through or around the massive ancient open cast iron works and then up a huge steep slope that took us onto other people's farmland. There were many different routes to Matfield from there. One took us through a cherry orchard which, in late summer and autumn, was the scene of an on-going battle between the farmer and the birds. He not only had 'bangers' that blasted out an explosive noise, but elaborate devices made of corrugated iron sheets and weights hanging from trees which created a colossal racket when you yanked on the rope.

Our destination on these journeys was a sweet shop which we called The Tin Tabernacle but which was actually called Sissons. It was along the Brenchley Road on the right as you headed out of Matfield towards Brenchley. The shop was run by Mr Mainwaring and on entering you picked up a little plastic bowl which you used to gather your penny and halfpenny sweets. They also sold a few toys.

CHAPTER 3

Matfield had two grocery shops at that time — one run by Mr McDonald, who was a serious man with a balding dome of a head and classic NHS glasses. He ran a very neat orderly, if rather sparsely provisioned shop and had a formal old fashioned manner.

The Badsell 'farmer's pool' 1971 (collection of Elizabeth Kirkor Rogers)

There was also The Cherry Trees Post Office and Tea Gallery opposite the butchers. This had a proper Post Office counter where Bill Waggit, in semi formal wear, was in charge. His wife Betty Waggit ran the tea shop in the large back area.

Betty was a special lady, a major part of Matfield life, and she did the best cream teas in the world. She had a pianola and a big tray of bizarre objects which she would bring out and challenge you to identify. She became very good friends with my mother after she caught me trying to steal a Flake - something which I am still embarrassed about today, especially as she would never let me pay for my cream teas. I console myself by reflecting that the incident lead to a great friendship. Mum and Betty shared a love of creativity and eccentricity and they even went on a trip to South Africa together.

Betty loved the theatre and had a close friend called Paulie who was openly gay which, in our narrow world, was unusual. Betty once memorably appeared as Britannia at an event at the Brenchley Memorial Hall, complete with breast plates, Union Jack and trident. She was a great story teller and claimed that the great operatic tenor Luciano Pavarotti's career had started in Matfield. Apparently he had been staying in the village, an impoverished unknown singer, as understudy to a major star who was performing at the Royal Opera House in London. This star became sick and Pavarotti's moment arrived. According to Betty she prepared sandwiches for him to take up to London and these sandwiches were of such exceptional quality they powered his performance, which blew the roof off the Royal Opera House and made him an instant star.

This idea that everything great somehow started in Matfield became something of a family joke and Mum, like Betty, had a tendency to make out that, dig deep enough, and you would find that Matfield lay at the root of most great things. Mum's other common saying was that you could 'go anywhere from Paddock Wood'. Now of course you can go anywhere from anywhere, but what she meant was that you could buy a train ticket to pretty much anywhere from Paddock Wood Station, which was sort of true.

Betty and her husband Bill were such an essential part of Matfield that it feels wrong today, when I am in the village, that they are no longer there. It also seems ridiculous that you can't sit down and enjoy a cream tea in such a beautiful village. Bill was a retired bank manager who dutifully manned the post office counter for more than 25 years, into his 80's. Like Betty he was a fan of the theatre and had seen John Gielgud and

CHAPTER 3

Laurence Olivier perform Shakespeare in their prime. He was a great fan of the Bard and he and Dad would occasionally get into a 'quote-off' - trying to outdo each other with memorised speeches. Bill acted as a judge when we organised a Shakespeare competition in the big barn at Badsell in 1994, where young people were invited to recite Shakespeare speeches.

Betty and Bill Waggit (Photo: Market Hill Photography)

In his latter years Bill enjoyed the peace of village life, listening to the cricket and watching it played on the Green. At lunchtime he would go across to The Star for a pint and today a brass plaque in the pub indicates "Bill Waggit's Corner".

Bill's peace was interrupted by two unwelcome intrusions. One was when Betty organised for him to go abroad to watch cricket in some far off land like India. On his return he made her promise never to send him away again. On another occasion the post office was robbed and they were held at gunpoint and tied up. Both BiIll and Betty showed true grit and their daughter, Sue, managed to get across the road to Mark the butcher, who called the police.

We made many trips to Matfield on foot as children and one autumn I went with my brother Rupert to a particular horse chestnut tree because we knew for a fact that it was producing a vast harvest of conkers. We took a little wooden waggon with bicycle wheels attached and had to climb into a heavily fenced space, covered in warnings about 'danger of death' due to electricity, as this was where most of the conkers had fallen. We filled the wagon to the brim with conkers and dragged it back to Badsell. Another time we found a huge dilapidated building off the Maidstone Road (now a house called Friars Mill). We started throwing stones at the windows and were accosted by a man on a huge horse wearing a black tailcoat and a top hat. He was in an absolute rage and I was terrified.

On another occasion, heading back to the farm with our sweets, we encountered the Bensons, some children we knew from our school, Derwent Lodge in Tunbridge Wells. They were William, Zoe and Samantha Benson and they lived on the edge of the village where Crittenden Road meets Foxhole Lane.

What ensued was a spontaneous playdate involving a very prolonged and enjoyable battle. I can't remember what we were all throwing at each other, possibly it was mud, but we lost track of time. The result was that Mum called the police. This business of calling the police happened quite a lot when we went off on our expeditions. It always filled me with terror as I felt there was a real chance of being flung into gaol.

Another time we took our bikes and headed down the drive and up Crittenden Road. I was so young I had a tricycle. Our plan was to make full use of the long steep road for a thrilling return ride. We were not in any way 'road safe' and we kept the whole expedition secret. In my memory Mum actually witnessed me shooting full speed down the hill. I'm not sure I even had brakes. It was the most furious I ever saw her.

When we were a little older we started walking to Paddock Wood which was a bit more of a treck - about five miles round trip. This took us a little way up Crittenden Road and then on a cross country footpath through orchards and past a pond where we would pause to hunt for frogs. We then traversed a cow field,

CHAPTER 3

where we learned the all-important skill of showing no fear to a herd of curious cows. After walking through a farmyard by the B2017 (Badsell Road) we would then find ourselves on what to us was a very busy road. Practically the first time we encountered it, we decided this was too exciting not to make something of it, so we started putting cans and bottles out on the tarmac to see what the effect of fast moving traffic was. After a short time the Police arrived and gave us a serious ticking off. The next part of the journey took us through the housing estate along Ringden Avenue before we joined the Maidstone Road which took us to the glories of Commercial Road.

Paddock Wood had a proper toy shop called The Toy Box, the very last shop at the end of commercial road on the left, and that was our principal destination. Rupert remembers this shop with great fondness. "My heart would beat faster as I opened the door" he says today.

The shop had a well stocked section of small rubberised dogs and that most prized item - the rubber silverback gorilla (complete, according to Rupert, with anatomically correct genitals).

Adam in front of the farmhouse with his tricycle.
'The Badsell Oak' is visible in the Park Field

The best part of the Toy Box, to be approached with reverence, was the 'joke' section where you could buy all the old classics - the chewing gum pack with a mouse trap mechanism, the mustard sweets, the fake dog poo. You could buy a cigarette that appeared to be real and actually glowed but there was another cigarette-themed item which came in the from of a tiny white pill. This had to be surreptitiously inserted into the end of a cigarette. We pulled this trick on one of Mum's great pals, Carolyn Carroll. She lit up her fag and soon the air began to fill with white flecks like tiny snowflakes. Rupert has never forgotten the wonderful sight of Carolyn, watching fascinated as the mysterious spectacle of 'indoor snow' unfolded, while continuing to smoke her ciggie with absolute assurance that it had nothing to do with her.

Rupert also claims to have bought 'Spanish Fly' in the Toybox. This was marketed as a surefire aphrodisiac and featured a badly drawn cartoon of a bikini clad woman swooning over a youth. Rupert got his hands on this substance and took it to a party. Now in his defence when Rupert 'spiked' a girl's drink (several times) at a party, it was in the hope that she would feel overwhelming love for him - not that she would pass out so that he could carry her away. In the event all that happened was that she complained of feeling itchy. Rupert's suggestion that he scratch her did not work.

What I loved was the vending machine outside the Toy Box that sold little plastic eggs containing a rubber toy called a Jumbly. These things appeared very briefly and I yearned for them for years. Other regular purchases were a bottle of Tizer as well as comics The Beano and Dandy (The Beano being by far the better one). I was a signed up member of the Dennis The Menace Fan Club.

I often just went off for walks on my own. A favourite destination was Pembury Forest where I don't remember ever encountering another soul. To get there I either walked to the end of the 'Sewer field' or the end of the 'End Field', a route that

CHAPTER 3

took me through a neighbouring orchard and then down a lane and past the sewage works, where circular treatment ponds were constantly watered by massive rotating arms. After that the track took you into Pembury Woods, where the pines had been planted close together but there was a system of wide paths. There were giant wood ants nests made of pine needles. The ants would quickly become enraged if you poked a stick in their nest. On one hot day I came across an adder basking in a sunny patch.

One of my cherished memories from those years was when there was a particularly heavy fall of snow and for some reason my parents were away. I went on a massive snow walk - roaming across surrounding farmland for hours. I ranged across Neil Wilson's land on the other side of the A228 and had the entire enchanted landscape to myself.

Of course we took the farm for granted as children and probably assumed everyone had the kind of freedom we enjoyed. On rainy days we were subject to the kind of boredom that every child of the 1970's was familiar with. There were only three channels on TV and on weekday mornings two of them might be showing the test card. The third channel always seemed to be showing a never-ending programme in which a weird American man showed two women various yoga moves. When we resorted to watching this we knew we had hit rock bottom. This would usually occur after we had played a few of Mum and Dad's records from their small collection. My favourites were a Goon Show record and Benny Hill's 'Ernie, The Fastest Milkman in the West'.

As we entered our teen years we started to go to discos at Brenchley Memorial Hall. Being the youngest, these events were always tortuous because, despite making every effort to look older, I was basically a child surrounded by assured pre-teens keen to get away from kids and assert their burgeoning maturity. Rupert and Emma were far more adept than me at making friends. In fact Rupert arrived at his very first disco and, as he entered, a girl took his hand and became his first girlfriend. It was Stephanie Webb and much later, at a party at Badsell, I enjoyed my first kiss with her sister, Samantha. Emma's first boyfriend was their brother Roscoe.

Emma with Simon

Rupert was always very stylish and as he got older he took more trouble over his appearance. This wasn't so much vanity as simply taking pride in how he looked but one Christmas, our Auntie Jill presented him with a mirror which had the words 'Yes Rupert, you look terrific!' emblazoned across the top. Rupert hung it in the bathroom and used it for examining his teenage pimples and brushing his hair for the rest of his years at Badsell.

CHAPTER 3

Damn building on the Tudely Brook. (Left to right Charles, John, Adam Wise, Adam, Sam Wise, circa 1980)

CHAPTER 4
THE WISEMAN FAMILY

The Wisemans were a big part of our lives at Badsell. Ernie Wiseman was born 3 April 1921 and Kathleen Abdi, his future wife, on the 25 July 1924.

They met down in Lambeth North underground station while sheltering from the Blitz during the Second World War. Before moving to Badsell they lived on the Waterloo Road in South London where their first son Kenny was born in 1948. Afterwards they moved to nearby Bazeley House where they lived first at number 25 and then at number 20.

Kath and Ernie Wiseman first became familiar with the Kent countryside when they worked picking hops, the closest thing they had to a holiday. By the time they came to live at Badsell they had two more sons. Brian was born in 1960 and Steve in 1962.

For many years Ernie Wiseman was the only full time employee at Badsell and Kath would come across the big front lawn from their cottage to the farmhouse to attempt to tidy up the chaos several mornings a week. Without her we would have all sunk under a mountain of mess. Her son Brian remembers that, after her morning's work in the farmhouse, Kath would

CHAPTER 4

walk back across to her cottage and say to him, "No matter how much cleaning I do over there it never makes any difference!"

Kath as a girl

Ernie had worked as a London rubbish collector, 'on the dust' as it was known, since he was a young man, collecting in the South London districts of Lambeth, Kennington and Brixton. His father had also spent his life 'on the dust' in the same areas and, as a young man, Ernie lived through the transfer from horse power to diesel trucks. He once told me that the day after the transition, all the horses were shot.

Ernie was an animal lover and he was still angry about it as he spoke to me several years later. That said, some of his attitudes to animals are shocking to modern sensibilities. He had a black cat called Lucky which went missing one time and it eventually emerged that she had had a litter of kittens in the straw barn down the drive. Before their eyes opened Ernie popped them in a sack and drowned them in a barrel out the back of his house. When his golden Labrador, Mandy, was on heat a boxer dog used to come from God knows where and sit out the front of their house waiting for his opportunity. Inevitably Mandy got pregnant and again the pups were disposed of. This kind of thing was common at the time.

Kath and Ernie on their wedding day in 1944

Initially the Wisemans would come to Badsell on weekends and holidays, staying with Ted Marsh in the first of the two cottages. Their son Brian remembers the day when his dad Ernie came home from work and announced, "I've had enough of this, we're moving down the country".

Kath was reluctant to go as she belonged to a big tight knit London family. She had five sisters and three brothers, one of whom, Freddie, visited Badsell often after Kath and Ernie moved permanently to Badsell in 1969. He liked to sit in the garden of the cottage in the summer, drinking a beer. Freddie had a job stoking the boilers at St Thomas's Hospital in London. This gave him ample time to read and he educated himself to a high level and was a fan of the opera.

CHAPTER 4

Freddie

Kenny was already 21 when his parents moved to Badsell. He had left school at fifteen and had been working for several years, including at the Automobile Association at their Leicester Square office. The move was a bit of an upheaval but he eventually loved being in the countryside and he got work with Halls, a Paddock Wood company that made greenhouses, before getting a job at the fruit importers, Pascual, where he worked for nearly 25 years.

Brian loved the farm from the start. He had kept hamsters and tropical fish in the flat near Elephant and Castle and used to be chosen to bring his school's pet rabbit home in the holidays. He would hide it from the landlord behind the sofa as rabbits were not allowed. Even today, in his sixties, his garden is a small zoo, lined with aviaries and animal cages.

When he moved to Badsell, Brian helped with the lambing and took to riding. A grey horse called Boris was kept in the field behind their cottage and he used to ride it daily, getting informal lessons from Mum. Rupert Hodges used to bring his ginger horse Copper to Badsell to make way for the hop pickers that came to Tattingbury Farm during the picking season. Brian was allowed to exercise Copper but one day it threw him and bolted all the way back home, running down the drive, up Crittenden Lane, crossing the A228, then along Alders Road, Five Oak Green Road, Church Lane and finally arriving at the Hodges Farm, a distance of nearly two miles.

Rupert with Brian and Steven Wiseman in the front garden of the Wiseman's cottage with Bert Howse's sheep visible in the Park Field

Brian had a lot of respect for his parents but it was Kath who was the strict one. If the three boys were fighting she'd pull out a bamboo cane and thwack them — in his memory it was him who always got the worst of it and it hurt like hell. I find it hard to imagine Kath hitting anyone. She had a lovely attitude to life.

She used to say that every day was Christmas Day because she had grown up in the kind of poverty that meant that luxuries like nuts and tangerines were only available on Christmas Day, whereas, in her later years, these things could be enjoyed all year round. She was a gentle soul with a big heart. She smiled easily and had a great capacity for laughter. She was often amazed or shocked and was always exclaiming, 'Oh my gawd!'

Kath at the front door of their Badsell cottage

Ernie carried with him a bit of old London - a world of horse drawn dust carts, hard graft, pubs with pianos and amazing characters. Mum and I once got him to sit down in his cottage and answer a load of questions about his life while I filmed him, an interview which is now an important piece of social history as well as a record of a great character.

GOODBYE BADSELL

Kath and Ernie celebrating their ruby wedding anniversary on the 9th December 1984 in the living room of their cottage at Badsell

Kenny with Brian's son Sean in the garden of the Wiseman's cottage

CHAPTER 5
THE PICKER WARS

During their early years at Badsell my parents had to negotiate a learning curve as they took on the challenge of farming the unforgiving clay soil. It was so sticky it would build up in great clumps on your boots. We leaned to 'kick' it off, usually aiming at a sibling.

At the beginning my parents rented the two largest fields to a man called Bert Howse who kept sheep and cattle on them. A man called 'Jacko' looked after them and the sheep were brought into the big Atcost barn for the lambing.

Ted, who was soft hearted, was shocked at how roughly the sheep were handled by Jacko, leading to one of his famous quotes: "He ought to treat them better," he told my parents, "after all, they're only human." Another of Ted's deliberate malapropisms was to describe someone as being "as rich as creosote." Both Ted and Ernie were essentially comedians. They joked constantly, producing an endless stream of banter and witticisms, many of which were old chestnuts.

Ted and Ernie

My father spent most of his weekends on the old Massey Ferguson tractor (forever known as Fergy), one of two tractors that they bought. The small size of these tractors made things like ploughing very time consuming. For a while my father's half-brother Ben Kirby came to stay from Cornwall and he too got stuck in. Ben fell in love with tractors and afterwards got a job with Heath Engineering in Horsmonden, but eventually he would answer the call of the sea and went off to be a fisherman in Cornwall. One legacy of his time at Badsell was that the little room half way along the main upstairs corridor of the farmhouse was forever known as 'Ben's Loo'. In his later years Ben treated himself, buying a tractor for use on the fields he owned next to the Helford River.

Initially Ted was the only full time labourer at Badsell and Ernie used to come down on the weekends, often with his family.

Ted's routine was that he would get up and have about six cups of tea at home. Then he would report to the back door of the farmhouse at seven where Mum would meet him and (in between keeping an eye on Dad's fry-up breakfast) they would

CHAPTER 5

discuss what needed to be done on the farm. Mum would then drive Dad to the station at Paddock Wood to catch the 8 a.m. train to London. At about 9 a.m. Ted would have what he called his breakfast and at twelve noon he'd have his lunch, which he called his dinner. Halfway through the afternoon he would have a cup of tea and he would knock off at 5 p.m. and have his 'tea' at home. He would then, apparently, have a snack before bed. This routine was the same for Ernie when he came to work at Badsell, although after a while the morning meeting moved from the back-door of the farmhouse to the yard.

Simon on 'Fergie' the tractor in the 1960s

Sadly Ted's wife died while he was still working at Badsell. He married again and lived for a while in Pembury but years of spraying Kentish orchards on an open tractor without a mask or any other protection caught up with him. He developed a blood disease and died while still relatively young.

Once Ernie was working full-time on the farm he quickly fell into a routine. At the end of the week he would get his wage packet in cash and he would hand it over to Kath. She would buy him a bottle of Bells whiskey and a couple of pouches of tobacco and as far as he was concerned, he was set up for the week. He drank his whiskey neat and would have a lager at lunchtime in the summer, but he didn't go out drinking and only went to the Queen's Head in Five Oak Green on Christmas Day. He loved being in the countryside and he grew every kind of vegetable in the extensive garden at the back of the cottage. As Brian puts it "he was well into it and he was good at it".

In the early years farming at Badsell was still quite labour intensive, certainly compared to today. The apples were tough to pick because it meant climbing up and down (and endlessly moving) immense 18-rung wooden ladders, all the time bearing an apple picking bag on your back. Pruning those trees took weeks. Later my parents planted small apple trees on the fields both sides of the drive and a pear orchard in a wide strip at the top of the west side of the farm.

My parents had some farm machinery but this was the last period of the small mechanised machinery that still requited a lot of manual work. Brian Wiseman remembers that the little combine harvester was only seven feet across at the cutter. Ted would drive and Ernie would stand up on a platform filling the sacks as the corn came down a pair of chutes. Brian often helped and my brother Rupert did too, when he was old enough. When the sacks were full they were tied off and kicked to the ground. Afterwards they would drive around with a tractor and trailer and pick up hundreds of sacks scattered all over the field - a hard day of physical labour. The sacks would then be emptied into wire bins in the Atcost barn, lined with thick sisal tarpaper.

The first straw bailer they had was also small and primitive. It released each bale individually, so afterwards the field was dotted with thousands of single bales, resulting in endless stop-start work picking them up.

By the time I was old enough to help with the bailing the

CHAPTER 5

machine left them in neat stacks. I knew I was really growing up when I could lift a bale on my own, although the bailer twine would almost cut through the bend in your fingers. By the time I was eighteen I could toss a bale up to the top of the full stack on the trailer.

Bailer twine played a big part in life on the farm. Anything that needed mending was usually tied up with bailer twine, which was either orange or blue and had a tendency to fray into separate strands. Being essentially plastic it was hard wearing. Dad occasionally used it to hold up his trousers and it was endlessly made use of in fixing and filling awkward spaces in the huge amount of fencing required in the 'pet area' when the place became a petting zoo. On one occasion, while quite a young child, I got myself into terrible pickle with it. I was balanced on a bale of hay with one foot raised up high and attached, with bailer twine, to a beam above. This was in the hay barn by the bullock barn, which later became the chicken display. I could not, for the life of me, undo the knot that I had tied and I was starting to get seriously exhausted — facing the prospect of hanging by the foot and possibly losing the limb. Luckily Steven Wiseman came across me and cut me down.

The Fergie tractor was open to the elements and we all learned to drive it. It was an incredible old workhorse that was second hand when we got it, served us for thirty years and was still working fine when it went to its next home.

The other piece of equipment that seemed to be there forever was a long flat-bed trailer with a thick rough wooden plank covering and no sides. We would load it up with the oblong bales to ludicrous heights, then all sit on the top as it wobbled madly on the return journey. This was terrifying when crossing the little bridge from the 'sewer field' (named because the Tunbridge Wells sewer works located about a mile further up the valley). Crossing this bridge was terrifying because, to save money, it had been built with no central section — the wheels of the vehicle had to line up with two concrete beams separated by a gaping hole looking straight down into the water below. If he was driving Dad always stopped at the bridge, refusing to go on until we all got off the straw stack.

Ernie bailing in the Park Field with kids Rupert, Steven Wiseman, Adam and Emma

We would then unload the bales and stack them carefully in the barn.

When we were kids the packed straw barn then became a play area and we would clamber about amongst the bales and the straw would creep down our necks.

The main game was to make a complex system of tunnels by shifting the bales about, and you would then crawl through the tunnels feeling a thrilling sense of mounting claustrophobia and occasional terror as you realised just how utterly disastrous it would be if a tunnel collapsed. The wonderful smell of straw was overwhelming.

When my younger brothers, John and Charles, became old enough to take part in this, rather than warning them off, I used it as an excuse to do it all over again and one day we had been

CHAPTER 5

crawling about through tunnels, mostly made by myself, when I came across a tunnel that had collapsed.

I could not find Charles and I started to feel rising panic as I contemplated the horror of being responsible for my brother's death. I started madly scrabbling about, ripping away at bales above where the tunnel had collapsed, and becoming massively over heated and half crazed.

The straw barn with Minnie the Jack Russell.

I could not find him but at some point I stopped searching and decided that there might be another explanation.

Could it be that Charles had simply wandered off from our game because he was having a bit of a craving? He knew he only had to go and knock on the door of the first of the two cottages (where our granny Ruth, known as 'Nan,' lived) and she would supply him from her always-ready sweetie jar.

This, as it turned out, was exactly what had happened.

After the cattle and sheep had gone my parents began by planting barley but gradually they branched out into other crops. The big development was when they planted strawberries which quickly led to them doing pick-your-own, which brought the public onto the farm.

Badsell was by no means the first place to do PYO strawberries but it was a very new phenomenon. Initially the weighing of the strawberries was done in the open at the edge of the field, with a set of little iron weights ranging from a pound down to a tiny half ounce, which would be balanced against the punnets of fruit. The money was taken out in the field too. People very quickly understood how PYO worked but families with children were always met with the same joke: "We'll weigh your children before and after to calculate how much they've eaten in the field."

A constant requirement at Badsell was for signage out on the road at the end of the drive and at other places such as the top of Crittenden Lane on the Maidstone Road.

John Rogers with Ted and Ernie in the strawberry field behind the stables (Circa 1970, Collection of Elizabeth Kirkor Rogers)

Dad would announce that we were going to sort out the signs and we would put an odd assortment of bits of wood, flattened cardboard strawberry trays, stakes, nails, bailer twine, a sledgehammer and something we called the allervanger (an extremely heavy iron object for making holes) in the boot of the Range Rover and head off down the drive. The signs themselves were hand painted or written using heavy marker pens. The writing on the signs was never particularly neat, there was a tendency for the 'font' to get smaller and smaller as it approached the edge, and the pens always seemed to be on the verge of running out. Eventually, when we opened the petting zoo, we created a big proper sign at the end of the drive which my mother decorated with a colourful painting of animals. An identical sign also stood near the yard.

Roland Rogers on the Honda three-wheeler in front
of one of Celia's hand-painted signs, circa 1986

As well as pick-your-own we always sent fruit to market, and the fruit tended to be picked almost entirely by women. These were often tough working-class Kentish women who brought their children with them. The kids would then roam freely about and, as a kid, they became my playmates.

Later my younger brothers, John and Charles, had a more antagonistic relationship with the picker's children. John remembers what he calls 'The Picker Wars'. To fight their battles John and Charles would attach old shotgun cartridges or nails to the ends of sticks and would project them at their enemies by swishing the stick through the air. After a while, they found a better weapon: burrs from burdock plants. These would become so horribly entangled that the affected hair had to be cut off. As John recalls it "the great mark of shame was if you turned up to battle with hair crudely shorn." Of course this all sounds a bit savage but when I challenge John about it today his reply is, "We were just emulating the behaviour of our older siblings, following the path you had carved out for us on the road of life."

When my parents first started growing strawberries at Badsell they managed to win a regular order from The Savoy Hotel in London. This was for their best fruit which had to be sorted and then driven up by Dad for early morning delivery. He would then go on to work — it was the days when you could just park all day on a street in central London. The Savoy used to sell all their food waste to a pig farm which lead to Mum learning one of her favourite pig facts. Pigs, apparently, are incredibly delicate eaters, with the ability to separate out even sharp fragments of glass in their mouths, then spit them out without doing any harm to their mouths. Her other pig fact was that pig eyes are almost identical to human eyes, something that used to freak me out when trying to outstare Gutsy the middle white.

Rupert by the farmhouse terrace with strawberries in the old white punnets.

CHAPTER 5

Another regular client was British Airways who bought our strawberries for their in-flight meals. Later I remember taking strawberries up to London with Mum. The Peugeot Estate would have all the back seats flattened and it would be packed to the roof with trays of strawberries. On a hot day the smell of warm strawberries in the car was intoxicating. Driving along on the A2 just before it hit outer London, Mum and I would chat away happily, the sun shining, the hard work of getting the fruit picked, packed and loaded all done.

In addition to strawberries we had a field of blackberries which grew along the banks of the Tudely Brook in the middle of the farm. Other crops we grew in quantity at one time or another were sweetcorn and Brussels sprouts, which were picked in winter. Mum always had a big vegetable patch on the go which produced an unlimited supply for the house in season, and often for the farm shop as well. Other crops we grew commercially were potatoes, oilseed rape and beans.

The Old Orchard produced colossal Bramleys, amongst other varieties, and the new orchard was planted with a range of apple varieties, of which we all became connoisseurs.

There were Coxes Orange Pippin (known as Cox for short), Worcester Pearmain, Discovery, Russet, and (a particular favourite of mine) Laxton Fortune. When I visited the farm with my father recently (almost thirty years after we had left the farm) we found that most of the 'little orchard' was now treeless but the little row of Laxtons was still there next to a row of black alder and tucked behind an ash tree. It was very late in the season but there were two Laxtons left on the tree. As soon as I bit into one I realised why I had loved this apple most of all. It has a subtle sweet fragrant taste.

Charles Preston

The pears we grew in the field at the north western edge of the farm, about half way down the valley, were Conference and Comice, both delicious when ripe. With both the pears and the apples we fought a constant battle with bullfinches which could strip all the buds from a tree in minutes. The way we fought this was to have male bullfinches in little cages, singing their hearts out to attract females. When one hopped in to the compartment next to the male she would be trapped. She would then be 'dispatched'. For a few seasons black cotton thread was draped all over the trees in both the apple and pear orchards. It was distributed by means of a light aluminium pole with several cotton reels attached. The theory was that birds would quickly discover that this invisible thread was everywhere and decide that the orchard was such an unpleasant place they would leave it alone. Of course the reality was they sometimes got tangled in it.

The battle to keep pests off the crops was constant. Another weapon in our arsenal was the 'banger' which was a light red and blue metal cannon. It was fed by a gas cylinder and it was on a timer. It was used particularly to protect the strawberries and the young oilseed rape from pigeons.

Every few minutes it would let rip with a massive bang and you made damned sure you weren't nearby to save your ears. As kids this was of course a thing of endless fascination — the most wonderful toy — and we used to stuff the mouth of the barrel with earth or even strawberries and watch it all blast out. Our parents were always telling us to stay away from it but we would gravitate back to it endlessly.

There were years when we had a 'glut' of apples - 1977 being an example. What this really meant was that the price of apples dropped because conditions were just right for a bumper harvest. At some point my father got involved with an effort to promote English apples as a direct response to the 'invasion' of the French Golden Delicious. The Apple and Pear Development Council was headquartered in Tonbridge Wells and had been set up in 1966 to promote English fruit.

Another aspect of this was that two local ladies, Theresa Wickham and Margaret Charrington, set up something called The Women's Farming Union to which my Dad acted as something of a mentor or, in his words, an *eminence grise*. They too got involved in the battle to save the English apple.

A lot of promotional material was created to counter the massive 'Le Crunch' campaign being organised by the French. One of our slogans was 'Polish up your English,' another was 'I'm an English apple eater.' These were printed on posters and paper carrier bags with images of English apples and pears bedecked with Union Jacks. We used the bags in the farm shop, which at that time was in the roundel of the oast house, and the walls were covered in the posters.

At some point my father started working at Dewe Rogerson, the advertising and PR company, and he actually handled the Apple and Pear Development Council account.

Soon I was recruited to help fight the good fight against the wicked French Golden Delicious. At one point I went to a protest in Trafalgar Square. I was given a banner to hold which read "Who Needs Frogs legs?" with a picture of two severed froggy legs drawn by myself in heavy black marker pen and coloured green. Even at that young age I sensed this was not particularly relevant or helpful — but I did end up on the cover of The Daily Telegraph.

One thing I never understood was why the Cox apple was chosen as the answer to the Golden Delicious. We grew a lot of Coxes on the farm and it was my least favourite 'eater'.

Coxes, eaten fresh off the tree, are hard and tart — not a sweet treat at all. I think they were chosen because they keep well in storage. Maybe their sweetness comes out over time but I only ever ate them fresh off the tree. Even my Dad, forty years after these events, admitted to me, "I never really liked the apple".

To promote the cox my father came up with the idea of going to the Oxford and Cambridge Boat Race. It was 1980 and a woman called Susan Brown was coxing for the Oxford team — the first woman to compete in the race in its 152 year history. Dad's idea was that we would go along and give Sue a box of cox apples at the end of the race and the press (who would be present in greater numbers than usual) wouldn't be able to resist mentioning it in their coverage because of the word 'cox.'

When it came to it Sue Brown's team won and there was a significant press presence, with hardened Fleet Street photographers barging each other about. I was 14 years old and during

CHAPTER 5

the key moment, when Sue and her 'boys' were posing and a great mob of photographers with big cameras were snapping away, Dad urged me to carry a big box of cox apples and give it to Sue. I started trying to move forwards, lugging the heavy box, but an oaf of a press photographer physically blocked me and gave me a look threatening violence. I did eventually manage to present her with some apples but I had a terrible sense that I had missed the key moment and the only publication that printed a picture was 'The Grower' magazine, which was read entirely by British apple farmers.

Adam presenting apples to Sue Brown, the cox of the Oxford team in the 1980 Oxford V Cambridge boat race

So immersed were we in 'apple culture' that at one point Mum, an amateur artist who had trained in Paris just after the war, got involved in creating a 'tessellation' of apples in Canterbury Cathedral. This turned out to be a huge undertaking, involving a vast amount of fruit that had to be very carefully sorted into different colour gradations so that Mum could 'paint' with them.

My sister Emma also did a lot of apple promotion, including dressing up as Nell Gwynn and singing outside Number 10 Downing Street.

Emma Morris and Emma Preston promoting English apples

CHAPTER 6
THE TWINS

When I was eight years old my parents announced that our family was about to grow.

I only have one very vague memory of seeing my mother pregnant on a sunny day when we were all on the terrace at the side of the farmhouse. This must have been during the summer holidays of 1975. At some point I must have been told that she was pregnant with twins. I don't think I reflected much on the reality of what this meant, until I was told to go upstairs and wait in my dormitory one day at Holmewood House, my prep school. My housemaster's wife, Mrs Simpson, came in and said, "Your mother has just given birth to twin boys."

This news stuck me as overwhelmingly joyful and exciting. The idea of twins just seemed to me to be absolutely outrageously amazing. I was already picturing them as a pair of Just William-style scamps and so distorted was my concept of time that I was sure that they would be coming to my school while I was still there. In my letter of congratulations to Mum I wrote that one of the teachers was 'terrified' that two more Preston boys were on their way.

GOODBYE BADSELL

John and Charles Preston, fresh from the Kent and Sussex Hospital, with Adam, Rupert and Emma on the terrace at Badsell

The first glimpse I got of them was through a viewing window looking into the maternity ward in the Kent and Sussex hospital. They were identical twins, exact genetic copies of each other, but within the family we could tell them apart from the very start. Other people have trouble telling them apart even today — when they are in their forties.

One of the family myths around The Twins is that my father threw a party to celebrate their birth while Mum was still in the hospital. When she arrived home with her new babies she found the curtains still closed and the air thick with cigarette smoke, the detritus from a boozy party everywhere. It is certainly true that my Dad was excited about being a father of twins. To him it seemed like something almost freakishly brilliant.

When The Twins were born there was a great deal of discussion about what to call these two new boys and a lot of ridiculous and pretentious suggestions were thrown about, but eventually they were christened with the solid English names of John and Charles at St Andrew's Church in Paddock Wood.

CHAPTER 6

Mum was quite lucky in that she usually had a nanny to help her with the children but I don't think she had one initially and she was always grateful to a friend of hers, Sally Hogg, who offered to come around and just take care of The Twins one night a week. Sally was probably the wealthiest friend Mum had, but of course however rich you are you only have limited time and she chose to give her time which was what Mum needed most.

John and Charles with Celia in the little room above the porch of the farmhouse which was their bedroom in their early years

When they were still quite young my father organised a 'twin party' to which he invited all the young twins in the area. The central event at the party was a competition to decide which were the most identical twins. The contest was held in the big Atcost barn and It was judged by our family doctor, Dr Baker. A pair of twins from my school, the Throwers, attended and, fifty years later, Mischa Thrower remembers the event, although in his memory it took place in a tent. Dr Baker selected triplets as the winners.

GOODBYE BADSELL

Local twins gathered in the Big Barn for the 'most alike' contest

In John's recollection he spent a lot of his early childhood waiting and watching the traffic go by on Crittenden Lane. The farmhouse was a long way from this road, meaning my parent's felt relaxed about letting them wander — and they chose to wander to the most dangerous place they could get to.

Eventually they came up with a solution of how to stop the traffic. they dragged logs and stones into the road. As John puts it "we pulled off the highwayman's trick of stopping passing traffic and hitting them up for valuables — which meant sweets," although it "rarely worked".

Charles remembers setting up camp by the stream next to Crittenden Lane in the woods. They found a cow's skull and a dead snake and this became their totem, with a candle burning inside the skull. From a very early age they embraced the idea of being the 'terrible twins'.

John's claims they 'lived' in the camp for two days and were eventually found by Mum who told them that they had missed a friend's birthday party. She was cross with them and yet the gift destined for this birthday child was given to them instead, offering a snapshot of how busy and distracted our mother was, running the farm and now raising five children.

The truth is The Twins spent many hours completely unsupervised and, not surprisingly, they got up to a lot of mischief and into a fair few scrapes.

One occasion, while still very young, they found their way into a shed being rented by Larry Marsh who was one of Ted Marsh's sons. He stored his work paraphernalia in there, which included his boots and a tin of green paint. The obvious thing to do, therefore, on a dark winter's evening, was to fill Larry's boots with the green paint. The result was that on the dark winter's morning that followed, Larry came in and put his foot in the boot.

When they tell the story now they claim that Larry was "a friend of the Kray twins" and connected to a "whole London fraternity of dangerous characters". In reality when Larry came to the kitchen door to report the crime he found it hard to be angry and had a glint of amusement in his eyes.

The Twins used to hang out amongst the nettles growing in the space after the end of the yard where the tar pit for the hop poles had once been located.

The tar pit was still there and was a sort of 'death pit' but what they really like to do was play with fire, something which had been a particular hobby of mine at the same age. John recalls that they used to fill water pistols with diesel, set light to the ends and use them as flame throwers. Eventually they would just stamp on them. When he was about five John miscalculated how long you could stand in the hot embers of a fire and his wellington boot melted around his foot. It was probably one of the worst injuries he suffered, but it did not require a hospital visit.

There was a dump at the farm and that was another popular place for The Twins to hang out. It was at the very top of the big orchard, slightly inside the sloping field by the woods, and constituted a large hole in the ground into which farmers had been throwing anything and everything for decades. The Twins established one of their many camps there and used to enjoy setting fire to asbestos and aerosol cans, both of which exploded, much to their satisfaction.

John (left) and Charles aged 12 months playing on the stairs in the farmhouse

The camp they built there was made chiefly of oil barrels which they packed together tightly so that it was almost hermetically sealed. On one occasion they imprisoned Joanne Miles in it, the daughter of a couple who had by then moved to the cottage that our grandmother Ruth ('Nan') had previously inhabited. They then threw in smoke bombs and shut the door. When I ask how she reacted the reply is "She was pretty good about it — but she cried and went home."

Years after Rupert had grown out of the den in the very top of the oast house, The Twins discovered it. The soft-porn playing cards were still up there and they started making a tidy sum selling them one-by-one to their friends at their prep school for a pound each. Unfortunately they were caught and they

CHAPTER 6

suffered the mortifying experience of having the headmaster show them to Nan who was horrified. It was the moment she realised her little cherubs were not innocent. They had transformed into black market porn merchants.

Of course having taken over the 'den in the sky' The Twins made it their own, decorating it with roadside paraphernalia including several reflectors and oil lamps pinched from road works. John even managed to get the road sign of the road his school house was on.

The den in the sky was witness to one of the more insanely dangerous things that The Twins got up to. They would climb out of the den through a louvred air vent and slide down onto the corrugated iron roof below. They would then jump about ten feet down onto the gantry. Finally they would drop down another ten feet to the ground. The problem was that this fun obstacle course initially involved squeezing past what John describes as 'like something out of Doctor Who'. It was exposed mains electricity equipment. Mark Lucas, who did building and maintenance work on the farm and knew a thing or two about the dangers of high voltage electricity, was so shocked when he saw what they were doing that he 'reported' The Twins to Mum. In the normal course of events Mark would never have 'dobbed' anyone in it for anything, being something of a free spirit — but he felt that this had to be stopped before someone got fried.

At some point The Twins were given brand new white catapults which, inevitably, turned out to be a very bad idea. Taking these weapons on their first proper outing they climbed into the small cherry tree that stood opposite the two cottages by the big lawn in front of the farmhouse.

Once ensconced in the tree they waited.

John (left) and Charles in the yard at Badsell with the Range Rover (Photo: Kevin Walsh)

Jose Dadswell had by then been a part of the Badsell 'family' for several years. She remembers driving away from the farmyard in her red Renault 5. She was just passing the large open-sided straw barn on the left when her back window exploded. The catapults had been loaded with stones and The Twins had let fly, giving it both barrels.

Speaking over forty years later The Twins still grow misty eyed at the memory of the "perfect shot" which caused the rear window of the red car to disintegrate.

The two boys then dropped from the tree and ran for it, disappearing up behind the stables towards what they called the 'Porter's Wood'. There they hid the catapults by a ditch before moving to some other part of the farm and acting innocent.

But Jose had seen them running and she reported the incident to Dad who asked for more evidence that his two youngest sons were the perpetrators (although it is hard to imagine who else he thought might have committed the atrocity). Once it was pointed out to him that they had seen them scarpering from the scene and they had recently been given catapults as gifts, he reluctantly accepted that his otherwise exemplary sons had done the deed and he coughed up for a new window.

After a suitable amount of time The Twins went back to collect their catapults from the ditch so they could resume the fun — but they found that the mower had cut them to pieces.

It is hard to say whether John and Charles were inherently naughty or whether there was a tendency to stamp them with the 'terrible twins' moniker which they then felt duty bound to live up to. I remember reflecting on this when I introduced them to a friend from school called Natalie Rae. Instead of shaking her hand one of them kicked her hard in the shins. I had a definite sense that he felt this was what was expected of him. On another occasion one of Lizzie Rogers' three sons, Roland, visited the farm for a few days with a girlfriend who, we were all informed, was a vegetarian. The poor girl was confronted with dead rabbits and pheasants hanging by the boot room and she was informed of the actual name of the pig we all ate that evening for dinner. On the second night we had rare roast beef and when Mum asked one of The Twins what he wanted as she served up the meat, he replied, "I'll just have blood please."

The Twins used to launch raids on a family called the Coles who also had twins, though they were of a milder and gentler character. Their house was along the Maidstone Road and was quite a long walk for two small boys but they loved to wreak havoc on this innocent family. Nick Sergeant, still a close friend of The Twins today, recalls preparing for one of these raids. They went into the Spare Room, the room to the left at the top of the stairs in the farmhouse which was kept immaculate for guests. "We decided to make a sort of bomb by squeezing ink cartridges into a bag. We used one of the beds as a surface and to protect it we put a plate face down on the cover but when we lifted it there was a huge circular ink stain. The attack went ahead anyway".

One of the things which The Twins enjoyed, which had not been around when we were kids, was a circus that came to live on the farm.

My grandmother, Ruth, used to drive The Twins to school in Tonbridge in the morning and by chance they discovered that a small circus was living in a field along the Heartlake Road near Tudely. Ruth used to make a small diversion so the boys could have a peek at the lion in its cage. One day they found, to their disappointment, that the circus had moved on, but when they got home they discovered why: it had come to live at Badsell.

Somehow the owner had got in touch with my father. He had turned out to be an ex-Royal Marine like Dad and had persuaded him that the circus would be an asset on the farm.

The man looked a little like an English version of Wild Bill Hickok but he turned out to be, in my father's words, 'rather lazy' and he would spend a lot of time seated in a chair near the lion cage claiming that this was necessary to get the lion accustomed to people.

The couple lived in a caravan which they brought to the farm and they were clearly down on their luck. The woman would walk the three miles to Matfield and return with two pig's heads in plastic bags to feed the big cats.

She kept anacondas in a basket and The Twins would go and visit her in the caravan after school. They would sit down and then, without fail, the woman would ask them if they would like to see the snakes. Of course they would say "Yes" and she would open the basket. She would find that the snakes were not there. A desperate search would follow.

It was a very small circus and there wasn't really enough for a full show, but for The Twins next birthday party it was agreed to do a performance in the Atcost barn, in lieu of rent. The man was rather an awkward Master of Ceremonies and he did a bit where he asked for a volunteer from the audience. A small boy was chosen, even though he clearly had no desire to be picked. The MC sat him in the middle of the ring, stood behind him, and announced that he was going to crack an egg on his head. The boy didn't like this one bit but the MC proceeded to tap the boy on the head so that he thought an egg really had been cracked and that his hair was now full of goo. He started to cry.

The other act I recall was the goat that walked the tightrope. This actually involved it walking across a plank while shitting itself with fear. Finally the woman, wearing a tight one-piece leotard, did an 'erotic' snake dance which fantastically inappropriate for an audience of small boys .

As Rupert, Emma, and I had done before them, The Twins took to walking to Paddock Wood when they were still quite small and they came up with an ingenious way of adding to their pocket money. In very busy shops, such as the newsagents, coins were often dropped during the course of the day. When they got to the till one twin would drop a small coin and they would both fall to the ground and pretend to search for it. In fact they were scooping up all the other coins that had been dropped by customers and had rolled under the counter.

When The Twins were around nine years old I began taking them on longer walks. We began with a walk from Badsell to Bewl Water Reservoir, a distance of about nine miles, almost entirely cross-country and using an Ordnance Survey map. We had good weather and went through glorious countryside. We talked continuously and seemed to have endless adventures and scrapes. At one point we came across a charming little shop where an old man was serving at the counter. I brought a pack of crisps to the counter and he said something like 'that'll be fifty pence" despite the fact that there was a huge clear label on the pack stating "40 pence'. However when I pointed this out he just kept nodding and repeating that it was "50 pence."

Charles (left) and John, hiking to Itham Moat in 1988 with St Gyles Church, Shipbourne, where Simon and Celia Preston married, in the background

Anything like this was a source of huge amusement to us but we managed to keep our laughter under control until we got out of the shop. Then a woman rushed out and gave us a severe ticking off. We then heard her explaining to the old man what had happened: "THEY WERE LAUGHING AT YOU" she roared, "I SAID THEY WERE LAUGHING AT YOU!"

When we got to Bewl we built our own shelter in the woods overlooking the reservoir. There were signs saying 'No Camping' and we had to climb over fences. We built the shelter using sticks and leaves but our one concession to modernity was a sheet of plastic. This was draped over a large sapling to create a basic 'bender'. In the morning we had tea with fried eggs, bacon and sausages and then we departed — leaving no trace.

This became our model for future hikes. Our rules were 'camp where it is illegal and leave no evidence'.

Our next hike was to Ightham Moat, a distance of about 10 miles, but the crowning glory in our adventures was a three-day hike around the Isle of Sheppey. Mum dropped us off at the

CHAPTER 6

Kingsferry Bridge and we just headed off in a south easterly direction with the intention of walking around the edge of the whole island.

Adam, John and Charles hiking to Heartlake Bridge, 1987

The east side of the island is a bird sanctuary and we walked all day in this strange flat landscape. At one point we came across an abandoned schoolhouse where we had our picnic lunch. That night we built our usual plastic sheet camp and then we headed to the 'PH' on the Ordnance Survey map. It seemed unlikely that there would be a pub as the area was so desolate and empty but we were praying that the map was accurate. We had brought our usual breakfast feast but nothing for supper and, after walking all day, we were starving. The other worry was — would they let two children into a pub in the evening? Of course none of these things could be checked in advance as neither mobile phones nor the internet had not been invented. Luckily the pub did exist, it was 'child friendly' and we had a fabulous and never-to-be-forgotten meal at 'The Ferry House'.

Day two of our Sheppey Hike was very different but also memorable. I do not think it is a secret that The Isle of Sheppey has suffered from questionable development. It is a place with three prisons and it has a lot of 'trailer park' type holiday accommodation. I am trying to avoid the term 'shithole'. But actually day two, which took us through the 'ruined' part of the island, has left me with a soft spot for dear old Sheppey ever since and I recently took my kids wild camping on the island. Sure enough they loved searching through the copious garbage on the beach.

During that memorable day we came across a theatre where Norman Wisdom was performing, at an advanced age, but the highlight was a very run down fairground. I paid £1.50 for the three of us to go on the 'ghost train' and as the attendant shut the door on our little open-topped carriage he took the fag from his mouth and said, "be prepared for a very dark experience." Not one feature of the ghost train was operational — we just shunted slowly through a pitch black tunnel. Rght at the end a tattered rag brushed over our heads, before we emerged blinking and laughing ourselves puce into daylight. That night we camped in the garden of an abandoned suburban house.

At the end of the hike we walked off the island to Sittingbourne where we found a tourist office. A very sweet little man gave us precise instructions for getting a train back to Paddock Wood. The Twins stood respectfully behind me while I extracted this information and I felt enormous pride that they were not giggling at the man's prominent hunchback.

Afterwards, walking along Sittingbourne's high street, I congratulated them on not giggling at the man's hunchback. "It's a real sign of your growing maturity," I continued, but when I turned to look at them they had both vanished. They had missed the hunchback and were running back to take a look.

One of the things that came out of these hikes was that The Twins took an interest in building shelters. When my parents

CHAPTER 6

moved to Bohemia, The Old Kennels near Frant there was a character known as 'Earth to John' who ran the 'Earth Spirit Festival' in woods nearby. He stored his yurts in the Old Kennels and John and Charles became fascinated by their construction. They built their own steam bender and created a yurt from scratch, doing all the sewing of the canvas themselves. The yurt they built became the first tent owned by The Bohemia Tent Company (now LPM Bohemia The Tent Company), who make and hire incredible tented structures and organise huge events all over the world. They provided the marquee for Prince Harry's wedding to Megan Markle at Windsor Castle in 2018.

John with Charles (seated) in the pet area at Badsell

CHAPTER 7
THE HUT IN THE WOODS

BADSELL WAS, AND REMAINS, RICH IN WOODLAND AND EACH one has its own atmosphere — each one drew us on different days for different reasons.

The small wood on the right as you enter the drive is dominated by a large pond. Tucked away behind it is an upwards slope followed by a hollow. For a while, when we were very young, Steven Wiseman and I used to go to this hollow and make fires and get up to all sorts of mischief. It culminated in our writing a letter to Zoe Benson, a beautiful girl who lived in Matfield. We were both in love with her but we made all kinds of lewd suggestions in the letter which we wrote anonymously.

It was quite a business for us to figure out her address and get a stamp. Neither of us had ever sent a letter before and it involved all sorts of subterfuge. I don't know what we were hoping to achieve but we were highly motivated. When the letter arrived at the Benson breakfast table on the edge of Matfield there does not seem to have been any need for detective work. Somehow everyone knew immediately that it was Steven and I who had sent the thing and we were permanently banned from hanging out together.

CHAPTER 7

The pond at the end of the drive had a sort of mythology about it. We told ourselves a story that a horse and carriage had once crashed into it and everyone had drowned. This might have derived from the true story of the loss of a cart at Heartlake Bridge near Hadlow in 1853 when 30 hop pickers were killed. It was certainly true that this pond was treacherous if you paddled into it in bare feet. I remember getting a nasty cut from some submerged metal. Norman Farnes, who was given the job of dredging out all the metal dumped in the pond, noted that something with the proportions of a car threw up bubbles from the centre of the pond, but it was too heavy to drag out even with a vehicle.

The same story was told about the area of bog land at the bottom of the Park Field which is reputed to have a sunken carriage in it. Now a pond, it is possible that this area gave the farm its original name of Bog Hole.

When the temperature dropped below zero we would head to the pond down the drive and tentatively put a foot on the ice before very slowly starting to walk out towards the middle. There would be deep loud cracking sounds and we got very good at telling if it was safe. We never fell through the ice and once it was properly frozen we would spend hours skating,

The other substantial pond on the farm is halfway up the sloping field in a small wood that juts out into the field. This wood was known to us as Solly's Wood. On one occasion the pond became frozen hard and we spent a memorable afternoon playing ice hockey with several of The Twins' friends.

Another significant wood on the farm begins after what was then the petting area. This wood lies either side of the stream and continues in a thin band following the stream before widening out after what was then The Blackberry Field. Here the Tudely Brook is fed by two tributaries. The left side one has more woodland around it and this woodland is special because the stream meanders, occasionally creating little oxbow lakes. Walking up this stream recently, with my own children, it struck me as being a true wonderland. Not surprisingly my favourite spot on the farm is there, where a mature oak grows on a steep bank, with a fox's drey amongst its great roots. Here, in season, you'll see banks of wild garlic and bluebells.

At my prep school I became obsessed with a writer called Denys Watkins Pitchford (known as "BB") and many of the scenes in books like *The Little Grey Men* played out in my mind as being set in this section of the Tudely Brook, making the experience of reading them almost hallucinatory.

Separating The Pear Orchard from The End Field is a thin strip of woodland known as The Shaw Wood which is believed to be ancient woodland, possibly one that has never been cut since the retreat of the Ice Age, 10,000 years ago. This is evidenced by the variety of trees on the wood which include the chequer or wild service tree.

The largest wood on the farm, Popreed Wood, is made up largely of hazel, ash and maple, but it is dotted with mature oaks. It used to begin with a row of pollard willows. The one just across the stream from the farmhouse was ancient and hollowed out at the base, forming a natural secret den which The Twins made their own, until they lit a fire inside it.

After this willow there is a narrow band of woodland following the north west edge of what was the Old Orchard. The bulk of Popreed Wood is then ranged across the top of the old orchard and the sloping field. In the top left corner of the old orchard an ancient sunken lane probably once brought timber and iron ore down to the valley for use by the iron foundry and farmstead. This track took you to the top of the Park Field where you could walk through to the top of the Sloping Field. To the right of this ancient path is a wide band of woodland and it was in the middle of this that my parents chose to create what

CHAPTER 7

became known in the family by the rather unimaginative name of 'The Hut in the Woods'.

The hut itself was an 'off the shelf' kit, which arrived as a pile of timber dumped at the top of the sloping field. This had to be carried into the wood along a path that we made for the purpose. This enterprise was incredibly exciting. We already had secret dens dotted about the farm but now we would have a proper secret shelter where we could spend the night.

The Preston family in the early 1970s in front of
The Hut in the Woods

The Hut in the Woods seemed to inspire people and others soon had their own name for it, perhaps reflecting their own dreams of utopia. My Godfather, Patrick Murchison, fell particularly in love with it and christened it The Nutcracker Suite while Ernie Wiseman called it 'Ponderosa'.

Patrick, a man of Irish descent, who was always known as

'Paki,' had been a wild character in his youth. He was full of fun and mischief - a joker who never fully settled to adult life. When Dad worked as head of PR at the London Stock Exchange, Paki would call up and ask to speak to 'Lord Bestiality Preston'. Paki was a big drinker and it probably didn't help that, when he did PR for Whitbreads, one of the perks was unlimited free alcohol.

Paki's escapades included once being arrested for leaving his radio and television on full blast in his London flat when he went away on holiday. It was his revenge on the neighbours who had complained about his noisy lifestyle. On his return he was sent to Wormwood Scrubs. On another occasion, in some foreign land, he found himself alone in an airport and had a panic attack which lead to him running through a plate glass doorway.

He was my Godfather and on one occasion he happened to be at Badsell around the time of my birthday. I encountered him in the downstairs hallway of the farmhouse and he reached into his pocket and gave me his loose change. At some point he became convinced that he and I were going to make our fortune by creating a filing system for people's record collections using specially printed cards. I did not realise that adults could be a bit bonkers and I became embroiled in this enterprise which involved me using transfer sets to create the cards. On his rare visits he would inspect the work and explain in detail why I had not got it quite right and needed to start again. During this period he was also managing a band called 'The Why'.

I think the The Hut in the Woods represented, for Paki, a dream of escape — a utopia in the countryside, off grid and away from the unceasing demands and responsibilities of adulthood.

On one memorable occasion he got drunk in London and took a black cab all the way to Badsell Park Farm, arriving at the farmhouse when my parents were out but we children were in.

CHAPTER 7

Rupert suggested they take a walk to The Nutcracker Suite where he kept him entertained until my parents returned.

Another evening Paki was staying in the hut on his own and Dad sent Rupert up to check on him. Rupert was only 14 but Paki plied him with whisky and even gave him a few tokes on a joint. When Rupert got back to the farmhouse Dad announced "Rupert we're going shooting and you're driving." Unable to admit to drinking whiskey and smoking pot, Rupert found himself driving the Range Rover around the farm while tipsy and high, with my father, Nico Rogerson and another man all standing on the drop down gate at the back with loaded shotguns. When they got down to the Sewer Field, Rupert drove too fast into a shallow ditch and when the back wheels hit the dip the vehicle bounced violently and all three men were flung off, loaded guns and all.

On the farmhouse terrace. (Back row standing from left) John, Patrick Murchison, Rupert. (Seated from left) Unknown, Adam, John Drake, Jessica Davies, Bob Little

I can remember the hut being built but I was too small to do anything but gawp and get in the way. We furnished it with two or three camping beds and a little camping gas stove. There was a butt to catch water from the roof.

Soon after we built the hut my parents very glamorous friends, Elizabeth and Nico Rogerson, came to stay and they asked to stay in the hut. She was a Polish model and he was the managing director of the very successful advertising and PR company Dewe Rogerson Ltd. I was quite young and I took Elizabeth a cup of tea in the morning.

Absurdly I walked all the way up to the top of the Old Orchard, across the top of the Sloping Field, and along the winding path through Popreed Wood carrying a little cup and saucer with tea in it. It was not even on a tray and not only was it cold when I arrived — it was about a quarter full. Elizabeth was very disappointed and announcing that she was going straight back to the farmhouse for a proper cup of tea.

When The Twins became old enough to get to the Hut in the Woods on their own they made it their 'centre of operations' and spent many nights there. Paki would come and stay and often camped in the hut with them, playing Radio Caroline late into the night. The old canvas bed that our Grandfather Frank had used in the trenches of the First World War was requisitioned for the hut and, by the light of the flickering candles, The Twins convinced themselves they could see bloodstains on it.

Central to The Twins idea of the hut in the woods was that it was secret and was not known to the other children who frequented the farm. A boy who was slightly younger than them, Nick Belton, the son of Gail Belton who ran the pet area for several years, remembers that he found the hut independently.

When he told The Twins that he had found their hut they initially denied that this was possible. They admitted that they had a shack in the woods, but that it was not the one he had seen.

They then announced that they were inviting Nick to stay at the real hut. When it came time to go they blindfolded him,

CHAPTER 7

only removing the blindfold to show him lethal mantraps which guarded the secret route. Nick was finally taken to the same hut that he had found independently — but by this point he was so terrified and intimidated that his eyes played tricks on him. He was convinced he was seeing a different building.

Nick got to build his own secret den with his friend Carl Browning down in the woods by the Sewer Field. He remembers staying practically the whole summer there. His mother Gail says that if Nick wasn't by the car when she was ready to go home after work she just left him.

When I got married to Liz in my forties I had grand ideas of having a vast stag weekend in a Scottish castle. Those plans were whittled down to just myself and my three brothers going back to Badsell and having tea at The Hut in the Woods. We took a flask and a cake and found that the hut had vanished — rotted clean away, with only a few odds and ends to show that there had ever been anything there. After our tea we retraced the old route to Matfield, which we had followed so often as children. The Wheelwrights pub was still functioning so we did a Matfield pub crawl — going on to The Star and ending up in what had been The Standings Cross and is now a gourmet restaurant called The Poet. Tame though this stag sounds, we were all thrown out of The Poet for bad behaviour just before midnight.

Growing up we also had a small light blue canvas tent which took a long time to erect. We would occasionally put it up by the Tudely Brook in the farmhouse garden where a patch of flat ground by the stream is sunk bellow the level of the lawn. One night in the 1970s my parents had a big summer party. Us and all the invited children formed a gang and hung out at the little tent which became our headquarters.

We noticed that grown-ups were occasionally walking alone across the lawn between the farmhouse and the outside buildings. We realised that there were so many of us that we would be able to overpower and bring down a single adult like a pack of dogs bringing down a stag. We started ambushing unsuspecting men when they were out in the middle of the lawn — attacking as a mob in a sudden unexpected rush, and dragging them down. It was fantastic sport because the men were reluctant to complain that they had been 'attacked by children', so they tried to make light of it. The game came abruptly to an end when we brought down a woman in a long 70's evening dress. She was absolutely terrified and her very angry husband came out and gave us a proper telling off.

On one occasion, when I was about 13, I pitched the little blue tent in the woods at the bottom of the Sloping field. Adam Wise, a local farmer's son agreed to join the adventure and I was amazed to discover that he was terrified of ghosts and needed constant reassurance. Adam is now a big burly successful farmer who owns most of Badsell's farmland. I think I may have teased him for his timorous behaviour in that tent nearly fifty years ago every single time I have seen him since.

CHAPTER 8
THE DOGS

Naturally, as we were on a farm, we always had a dog. When I was very young we had a dachshund called Lollypop. Tragically she gave birth to a single still-born puppy, which struck me at the time as unbearably sad. I also recall when she had to be put down, having reached a great age, and it was the only time I saw my mother cry.

Rupert on Fergie the tractor with Lollipop

After that we had a series of Jack Russells, the first of which was Pippin. I was very close to Pippin and could spend hours lying on the carpet in the downstairs hallway enjoying the intense connection that exists between children and animals. I could also work her up into a frenzy by spinning her around on her back and generally whooping her up until she would start darting around at high speed, having an attack of 'the scoots'.

We had a distinctive door buzzer in the Badsell farmhouse and it always got the dogs barking but no dog was quite like Pippin when someone came to the door. She would shoot down the hallway or along the upstairs corridor and down the stairs like a bullet then launch herself at the door and hit it with a loud 'crash'.

Adam with Pippin on the farmhouse terrace

She liked to sneak off to Mum and Dad's bedroom and spend the afternoon under the covers, her curled up body visible on the otherwise perfectly made bed, like a hillock on a plain.

Our dogs were very lucky because they had complete freedom. There was no busy road so they could come and go as they pleased through the dog flap in the back door which was never locked. The only time they were kept inside was when we burned the fields after the harvest.

As more and more animals were added to the place whichever dog was resident in the house rose in status as the 'chief animal on the farm'. Luckily none of them were chicken killers

CHAPTER 8

— if they had been there would have been constant chaos. Family friends Sandra and Allan Gardener once came to visit with two long haired Dachshunds which had never seen chickens before and they launched themselves at the bunch of free roaming chickens known as the 'Street Gang'. It was the only time those chickens ever took to the skies and one of them, a cockerel, ended up on the roof of the Atcost Barn.

Pippin lived a full and long life but suffered a tragic demise. While we were on a skiing holiday one Christmas we left my grandmother, Ruth, in charge and she was out walking Pippin on Christmas Day. She encountered a neighbour walking her greyhounds. She was a lady with lank blond hair, who always seemed to have a fag in her mouth and her own little private swarm of flies buzzing around her head. Her greyhounds went for Pippin as though she were a rabbit and she was badly bitten, puncturing her lung. Poor Nan had the worst Christmas of her life and Pippin died soon after our return.

Another Jack Russell, also a rescue, this time called Jane, had a very volatile temperament. If you moved too quickly near her she would grab hold of your trouser leg and not let go. She would then shake her head and growl and try to tear your trousers off. She once succeeded in entirely removing Charles' pyjamas so that he was left completely naked in the downstairs corridor. The only thing you could say in Jane's favour was that she was anti smoking. If she could get hold of a packet of cigarettes she would tear them to shreds.

Jane became very sickly and was taken to the vets. The X-ray showed a birthday candle holder was blocking her intestines. We held many children's birthday parties for members of the public in the café and likely it came from one of these. The object was removed in an operation but by this point she was so weak she did not make it.

With 'Lady' on Camber Sands (left to right)
Charles, John and Celia (Photo by the author)

Our third Jack Russel was also a rescue, this time called Lady, who also died prematurely. Having a large number of chickens meant that we had a constant battle with rats and she managed to get at some rat poison and ingested it — despite the considerable care that was taken to make it 'dog safe'.

After this my sister Emma went to the Traveller site at Cinderhill and chose a Jack Russell puppy. She fell for Minnie, as she was soon named, because she was a bit of a runt, with a slight squint. Unfortunately she did not collect the dog on that first visit and came back with a friend called Toby Treves who drove an open topped sports car called a Frog Eyed Spright. On seeing the fancy car the Travellers upped the price considerably, but by then Emma was besotted and the dog was purchased.

Minnie had a tendency to bite little girls in white socks. Not surprisingly, as we were a petting zoo catering to small children,

CHAPTER 8

this happened many times yet somehow no child ever got seriously hurt and we were never sued. What is more she didn't restrict her biting to small children. Nico Mead who came to work at Badsell in 1992, at the age of 13, was scared to go across to the farmhouse to collect her wages because Minnie would chase her and bite her ankles. Nico's sister, Carlie, had the same problem later when she came to work in the café. Occasionally she would have to walk across to get something from the farmhouse kitchen. She learned to keep a pair of Minnie-proof Wellington boots in the café.

Celia with Minnie (John in the foreground)

My mother adored Minnie and would become distressed if anything happened to her. On one occasion she went missing completely and when all searches failed we put the word out that we would pay a £50 reward for information leading to her return. A couple of Travellers arrived with her soon afterwards.

One time Gail Belton remembers Mum calling out, "Gail, Minnie's dying!" It turned out she'd got a stick wedged in tight across the roof of her mouth. Minnie was making a big fuss about it but nobody wanted to help because, "We knew we were gonna get bitten," as Gail puts it.

One day Mum went for a walk accompanied by a strange woman who had come to one of our many parties. This woman claimed to be able to speak to animals. She accompanied Mum and Minnie and after walking around the whole pet area she announced, "Lopez the llama is not happy, and your dog doesn't like her name."

Despite this Minnie lived to a grand age, ending her days at Bohemia near Frant where my parents moved after they sold Badsell.

Probably my favourite dog from Badsell days was Jessie.

While working at Transatlantic Films in London, the company secretary (a dog lover), showed me a list of dogs that needed to be re-homed. There was an entry for a dog called Jazz who was living in Hammersmith and had, according to the description, grown too big for her adoptive family to cope with.

I went to visit Jazz and found a huge half-Labrador half-great Dane. Her current owners, a London cabbie and his family, loved the dog but she refused to stop growing and it had got to the point where, when she tried to change direction in their little downstairs corridor, she had to do a three point turn.

I told Mum about Jazz and she drove up in the blue Badsell van to collected her. When we arrived at the farm I let the dog out of the back and she saw wide open space for the first time in her life. You got a sense of animal feeling enormous joy at discovering that there was this thing called 'the countryside'.

We decided that 'Jazz' was a bit of a naff name and changed it to Jessie (after Jessie Norman the opera singer). She was a wonderful-natured dog, with a loving, calm aura and she seemed to really appreciate the good luck of finding herself on a farm. Not surprisingly, however, she did not understand that our animals were not there to be hunted and killed and unfortunately she was a sheep chaser.

This was a serious problem and it came to a head one summer evening when Mum was in the house alone and Jessie chased one of the Wensleydale sheep. By this point Jessie's

CHAPTER 8

sheep chasing had been going on for a while and Mum went and got the twelve bore shotgun.

Jessie had brought the big Wensleydale ram down in the stream near the house and was about to savage him when Mum aimed and fired. As she put it "I was all on my own, I didn't know what else to do".

Jessie on the front porch of the farmhouse

Jessie released the sheep and ran away. The sheep got to its feet unharmed. Mum, naturally enough, was upset and called the vet who advised her that pellets from a twelve bore shotgun are red hot and therefore do not carry infections into the body. In other words, if the immediate damage didn't kill her, the dog would live. Mum was worried that Jessie was never coming back anyway — but when she went to the back door she found Jessie curled up in her huge wooden bed, bleeding heavily from the ears.

Jessie made a full recovery although you could feel the little lead pellets embedded in her ears ever afterwards. Bizarrely my mother also had bullet fragments embedded in her body — from an accident in Arizona. At a fiesta a cowboy discharged a shotgun, embedding a handful of lead pellets in her bum. Ever afterwards these would show up on X-rays and sometimes even set off alarms at airport security.

We also had a dachshund puppy called Solly for a while. One day Dad was tending a fire in the wood that juts out into the sloping field with John and Charles who were about six years old. At some point they became aware that Solly was missing. Some believe the dog went down a hole and became overwhelmed by heat or smoke.

Male dachshunds do have a tendency to run off, particularly when young. If he had done there is a vast woodland near where he disappeared and he may well have simply failed to find his way back. A search was launched involving every friend we could persuade to come to the farm — but Solly was never seen again.

Ever after the wood was known as Solly's Wood.

Emma with Solly

CHAPTER 9
"CAN YOU JUST GET THAT BUCKET?"

GROWING UP WE OFTEN WORKED ON THE FARM ALTHOUGH we also always had a sense that we were not doing enough. I remember Mum getting furious with me when I was complaining about being made to undertake some repetitive task involving endless kneeling and bending over in a muddy field on a freezing day. I just wanted to go and eat buttered crumpets and watch a Carry on film.

I planted strawberries (each plant had to be first dipped into a special liquid) and potatoes — a job I liked because you sat on a tiny seat and dropped each potato down a tube as the whole thing was dragged behind Fergie the tractor. The potato planter still stands, now a decorative antique, halfway up Badsell's drive.

One winter I spent a lot of time picking Brussels Sprouts in the freezing cold and my hands became hardened to the point that I could sheer the sprouts off by running my thumbs down the stalks.

There were some jobs we enjoyed more than others. We could generally be persuaded to get involved with burning the apple prunings — a classic winter weekend activity. Afterwards there was a huge glowing pile of red hot ash. Kids love a fire and of course this was one job where you could stay warm. We were always playing with lighted 'torches' and we cooked Bramleys in tin foil. We had an apple corer and you would fill the hole with raisins and brown sugar.

Strawberry planting on The Old Orchard

We could always earn money on the farm if we wanted to. I picked a lot of strawberries for which I think we were paid a pound a tray. A tray took a long time to pick and it was slow and uncomfortable. You had to admire the women who would pick all day, day after day. Some were incredibly quick and were highly prized as workers. Eventually I learned that the key was to be quite rough with the plant and pick every single strawberry on each plant.

Strawberries are a thirsty crop and a lot of time was spent working on the irrigation. Of course Badsell had a stream and the pump would be submerged in one of its deeper sections and the water pumped up to a series of long rigid aluminium pipes which were joined by rather awkward devices. You had to twist the whole pipe to either couple or uncouple it from the next pipe. To join two together they had to have opposing fittings. The worst job was laying out and fitting the pipes from scratch

CHAPTER 9

as you were always searching for a pipe with the right end, and twisting them on sometimes just twisted them off from the other end!

After the strawberries had been picked they had to be prepared for market. This was paid by the hour. It involved checking that each punnet contained consistently sound and ripe fruit and that it weighed half a pound. Then we used the 'overwrap machine' to wrap cling film over the top. You pulled a length of cling film over the top of the punnet then lowered the film over a red hot wire which cut the film neatly so you could tuck the loose film underneath. The problem with this job, which I remember doing for hours and hours, was that inevitably you would burn yourself on the hot wire. It was agony and left little burn marks on the ends and edges of your fingers. Rupert remembers doing this job while playing the Harry Lime Theme from The Third Man on an old wind-up 78 record player.

Elizabeth Kirkor Rogers with the potato planter
after it became an ornament on the Badsell drive

One year the fields of wheat were badly infested with wild oats and Dad declared that he would pay us half a penny for each wild oat plant we collected. This seemed like easy money until we got to work. I remember counting out a great fat sheaf of them. I had been working for hours — but had earned less than ten pounds. Of course I wanted to help the crop as well — but I remember going down to the sloping field and seeing how much wild oats were growing there, and realising that it was like trying to hold back the tides. I think I quietly went back, took my wages, and didn't mention what I had seen.

Another year Dad announced that blackthorn bushes were carrying a fungal disease that caused blossom wilt in fruit trees and we had to grub them all out. My schoolfriend Johnny Drake was staying at the time and we were put to work. Of course we liked a bonfire but blackthorn has huge thorns. Trying to work your way to the base of the trunks so that you could saw them down was a nightmare — with the thorns easily penetrating leather gloves. It was another occasion when I kept quiet on discovering, on day two, what seemed to be a whole woodland of solid blackthorn. Whatever threat these bushes posed never actually came to pass anyway.

As we got older we were given more responsibility. One year Mum and Dad went on holiday to Brittany leaving us kids alone with Janet Poile (now Weir) looking after The Twins. It was the time of the blackberry harvest. There were about ten long rows of them and Rupert was given the job, aged 16 or 17, of overseer. This involved hanging out by the waggon where the blackberries were loaded up, weighing and checking the trays as the pickers brought them in, and chalking up their totals.

Almost immediately Rupert took charge there was a revolution. The crop hadn't been as plentiful as in other years or possibly they were trying to take advantage of his youth, but the older pickers demanded more money. They were mostly grown women and some of them were pretty scary, although Davina, whose breasts were so formidable she could balance a tray on them while she picked, was only about 14.

They were paid one pound a tray and they wanted one

CHAPTER 9

pound twenty. I am not sure what the outcome was but the situation then descended into farce. Some of the younger pickers, including Davina, ganged up on Rupert and went after him, running him down and then using the heavy black marker pens he used to write on the blackberry trays to draw hearts and 'I love yous' on his chest. All this undermined his authority badly.

Although we kids did help out we were also keen to do our own thing. As teenagers we became adept at hiding — if you were seen you would be grabbed to fill a gap in the complex array of activities that were going on. Despite a large and ever growing work force, particularly at the height of the season, there was always the sense that the situation was slightly out of control. You might find yourself working the till in the gift shop, over wrapping strawberries, or dealing with some kind of emergency in the pet area. One time I heard Mum cry out that the ferrets had escaped and I ran like hell, with visions of a ferret having closed its jaws on a child's hand (they are notorious for never letting go). When I got to the cage the ferrets were innocently going about their business.

A common order would be 'can you just get that bucket.' With so many animals being fed in different places there always seemed to be a need for a bucket somewhere or other.

'Just get that bucket' became a running joke between my older brother Rupert and myself. If I was in my room my brother would shout upstairs 'Adam can you just get that bucket' as a matter of course, just to be annoying. I remember early one morning looking out of my bedroom window, three floors up, and seeing Rupert walking across the lawn, actually carrying a bucket. "Rupert can you just get that bucket' I shouted - and he looked genuinely annoyed ."Oh I see you are already getting it." I added.

Probably my favourite place to 'escape' was the Porters, our wonderful neighbours whose house was set back from the A228 and was a walk of about a quarter of a mile from our house. This involved walking to the top of The Horse Field, then through a small wood and across another field. The Porters consisted of three daughters, Pip, Gilly, and Joe and parents Sue and Richard. They not only had a swimming pool (a proper one, not a hole lined with black plastic) but the pool had a diving board from which I did 'Hong Kong Phooey' dives. The Porters were incredibly generous and allowed us to swim any time - without even needing to call and check.

The Porters also had a special room for watching TV and — more importantly — a video player. Whereas in our house watching TV in the daytime was forbidden, Sue was highly indulgent and would let us gather in this snuggery with cans of Coke and we would watch the latest movies rented from Blockbuster in Tunbridge Wells or, later, Paddock Wood's video shop, even on a sunny day. It was there I watched all the Monty Python Films and classics like Taxi Driver and Stir Crazy.

After the wheat, barley or oat harvest the straw would be turned into bales and then the stubble would be plowed back in — but if the barn was full of straw and the price for bales was low we would burn the fields.

For me, as a boy, this seemed like the most insanely fun thing to do. I was a pyromaniac anyway and used to spend hours in the huge fireplace in the farmhouse, staring at glowing embers and experimenting with burning and melting different things. For a kid with a love of fire the farm was a bit of a paradise. We were always building bonfires and in those days nobody cared about toxic fumes or the impact of burning things like rubber tyres or empty plastic fertiliser sacks. One favourite thing to do was to burn these plastic sacks and dip a stick into the melting, burning plastic. You then held the stick up and the hot burning dripping plastic made cool sounds as it fell to earth.

Even more amazingly I was allowed to help burn the fields

CHAPTER 9

in my very early teens. Nowadays, if burning fields was even allowed (which it isn't), any kids would be taken off site to get them away from the dangers. The only safety measure we enacted was making sure the dog was shut up in the house, much to its annoyance.

When the burning started I learned to gather a sheaf of dry corn stalks, light one end and then, pressing the burning fronds into the lines of dry piled-up straw left by the combine harvester, walk along, spreading the flames.

Within seconds the landscape was alive with fire. It was always done against the wind, to stop it running wildly across the field and then leaping into the woods — but on several occasions the flames leaped into the woods anyway and the fire engine would be called.

However, regardless of whether the fire engine was called by us, someone always called them anyway. Somewhere, somebody would see a massive column of smoke rising and assume some tragedy was unfolding. I got the impression that the firemen spent a lot of their time, at that time of year, attending field burnings on farms in the area. We always gave them beer and there was a sense that, for them, this was all a bit of a jolly, or at least a relatively relaxing way to spend a few hours. There was one occasion when the flames leaped into the wood at the very top of the Park Field and the firemen had to put it out. The only other time the firemen had to do anything other than drink beer was when a couple of the lads who worked in the shop managed to set light to a straw stack half way down the valley while having a cigarette — although I don't think there was much they could do about that.

When we burned the fields the straw lay in light piles, so it never got particularly hot. It burned quickly leaving black ash with a distinctive smell that, when I occasionally sniff it, takes me back to my childhood. Another distinctive smell came from the small piles of spilt corn that had burned, creating an aroma of raw toasted flour.

We loved to leap over the burning piles of straw and occasionally you would misjudge it and land in the flames. Speed was the simple solution and you just leaped out again — the flames never had time to do any harm. However, occasionally, you would get too close to a roaring wall of flame for slightly too long and you would feel your face 'burn' momentarily. Afterwards I would be red faced and lightly grilled.

Running about on the hot black ash, just after the flames had passed, gave you a sense of being in another world. It felt like no man's land after a battle, or a land blasted by some awful catastrophe like a volcanic eruption.

People probably assume that a lot of wildlife was killed by these fires but I never came across a dead field mouse or any other animal.

The burning of the fields was sheer heaven. What was so exhilarating was the sense of anarchy, the feeling that you had broken a sacred rule: you do not set alight to the world.

Later, when The Twins were youngsters, they too got to burn the fields. Mark Lucas remembers driving the Honda three wheeler motorbike across the stubble at high speed, dragging a burning tire, with both the twins as passengers. Afterwards they were blackened from head to toe. The Twin claim they also did this without Mark Lucas and that, having crossed the field, they braked and the burning tyre flew over their heads and landed in front of them.

If there was a favourite time of all during the Badsell years it was probably the summer of 1976 when there was a heatwave. At some point during our three month summer holidays, I stopped bothering to wear shoes and my feet became so hardened I could even run through the stubble after the harvest.

Days merged into each other and, with clear blue skies and

CHAPTER 9

Mediterranean heat, the farm became even more of a paradise than usual. The holiday seemed to go on forever and I forgot even about the existence of school — as did my parents.

(Left to right) Emma (holding Pippin), Steven Wiseman (holding a mouse that had run up his trouser leg), Adam, Rupert

One Monday morning we were out playing in the Park Field when we heard Mum shouting, calling us into the house. It emerged that the new school term had started that morning - Rupert and I were meant to have gone back to Holmewood House the night before. Brutally and abruptly the holiday was over and we were driven straight to school and had to walk into the middle of a class.

CHAPTER 10
THE PET SHED

The 'pet shed' was a large shed with a corrugated iron roof built onto the back of the great long bullock barn which would later house goats, a cow and other larger animals. The first person to use the shed was Brian Wiseman who kept his lovebirds in an aviary. Throughout my early childhood it was where we kept out pets - at first some rabbits and later ferrets and chickens. Once the petting zoo opened it hosted a variety of animals - from giant stick insects to a colony of gerbils who lived in a glass tank full of sand.

Down one side of the pet shed was a wide shelf at about waist height, which must have once had some kind of agricultural use. Because we fed chickens in the shed there were always a few mice about. You would rarely see them but one day I was sitting on a bale of straw with my chin resting on the shelf when a mouse came out, walked right in front of my face, paused, picked up a grain of corn and ate it inches from my eyes. I was not moving so it did not regard me as a living thing. After that I sat transfixed — watching mice go back and forth and cavorting about.

Although we regarded ourselves as country people we were

CHAPTER 10

not really part of the 'hunting and shooting set'. That said my Mum and sister, Emma, did go fox hunting often and the rest of the family would tag along. Emma was actually blooded at age 8 on her pony Willy at a hunt at Eridge Kennels where, half a century later, my father lives today.

For me a fox hunt usually meant driving pointlessly around the countryside, catching occasional glimpses of the hunters and then going to a pub for lunch. As far as I could tell the hunts almost never caught a fox and it was really a sort of ritual that got everyone out on their horses ranging freely across the land. I never saw a kill and Mum would generally tell me that the hunt had been unsuccessful. However she knew I adored foxes so she may not have been giving me the full picture.

Emma with her pet rabbits

We did not go to pheasant shoots as actual shooters but Rupert and I were sometimes asked to go along as beaters. This was hard work, involving a huge amount of walking. You had to yell and smash a stick against trees and undergrowth, driving the birds towards the guns, and at the end you would get lunch and £5 or, if you were lucky, £10.

Our main 'blood sport' was ferreting.

Rupert was the first to get a ferret and after that they played a big part in our childhood. My sister Emma always claims I 'stank' of ferrets until I was eighteen. Ferrets do give off a fierce pungent stink. They are lithe, active, potentially vicious creatures. The first things you have to learn to do, if you are a ferret owner, is pick them up just behind their front legs so they can't bite you. Of course a ferret that is well treated and handled often will not bite you, but it pays to be careful.

Adam with his ferrets

The ferret cage was built into the pet shed opposite the door and to the left of the large aviary that Brian Wiseman built for his lovebirds. Later this large floor-to-ceiling cage would house my pet fox. Having ferrets living in such close proximity to chickens was a little hazardous but only once did a ferret escape and get hold of a chicken and I did manage to rescue it. By covering the ferrets nostrils it was forced to release the bird which was unaffected.

The ferrets had a series of narrow ramps, with little grips in

CHAPTER 10

the form of batons, which allowed them to climb up to the very top of the cage. We fed them on a mixture of dog food and bread, eggs and milk. Ferrets are relatively tidy creatures who always defecate in the same corner, but cleaning them out was never pleasant. If you let things slide a bit, as we inevitably did as children, the build up of poo could be challenging. Mom was always telling us to "clean out those bloody ferrets!"

Sometimes I would take a ferret into the house and let it explore. It was fun because they check absolutely everything out — put them in a cupboard full of toys and they will go through it as though they had been sent in to search for a pin. After a while the excitement of it all would cause them to get the 'skits'. They would arch their backs and make funny little high pitched noises, leaping in the air and snapping their jaws. Unfortunately, at some point, they would do a poo on the carpet. I think because we often gave them milk, this poo was almost always loose and very hard to clear up. I can remember trying to clean up one of these disasters in my sister's bedroom and I could not get the smell out of the carpet. Being a kid I decided the answer was to spray perfume on it. The combination of ferret poo and Opium perfume remains, to this day, the worst smell I have ever encountered.

When I was about seven I started going ferreting with my brother Rupert. We had an old wooden ammunition case from the First World War - a relic of my Grandfather's time (Frank Thornely fought at the battle of the Somme on his 19th birthday). The ferret would go in the box with a bit of hay and we carried the ferret nets in a khaki canvas rucksack.

We were hunting rabbits and when we found a suitable warren we would set a net at each hole. Each net had a little wooden stake which we drove into the ground with a mallet. We never had enough nets and they had a tendency to become horribly tangled.

If a rabbit came out of that hole the net would close around its body and you had to then grab it, disentangle it, and break its neck. I have become soft hearted and I would not do this now — unless out of necessity, when the zombie apocalypse comes.

Netting a large warren took ages and often you had to contend with nettles and brambles, inaccessible burrows in thickets or huge, awkwardly shaped burrows that required you to pin parts of the net up with sticks.

Once we were sure we had netted every hole we would take the ferret out and place it in the mouth of a burrow, holding that net aside. The ferret would sniff about uncertainly and then usually, taking delicate little steps, make its way gingerly down the hole. We would then readjust that net and wait.

There were of course a lot of rabbits living at Badsell and their nibbling of crops probably cost the farm a great deal — but there was little pretence that we were 'hunting vermin'. This was hunting for sport. The only thing I would say is that we were not very successful. Most ferreters have a dog that tells them if there is a rabbit down a hole. We always had a Jack Russell but they were not trained and we did not take them with us. Without such a dog you would spend hours unknowingly netting empty warrens, and every time you released the ferret down a hole, you never knew how long it was going to be before you saw the animal again.

On mid-winter days we sometimes spent hours squatting by holes waiting while our toes turned numb with cold.

The most common outcome was that, after a while, the ferret would appear in the mouth of another hole. When this happened you had to catch the ferret which was not always easy. The ferret did not want to be caught and would choose either to run back down the hole or attempt to make a run for it into the woods. If you failed to catch the ferret a few times it

CHAPTER 10

would get the 'scoots' and would shoot back down a hole if it caught sight of you.

The ferrets were mostly white with pink eyes, or occasionally they were 'polecat ferrets' with a browny tinge to them. I had a favourite for a while, called Jinx, who was a polecat. He was dark brown, stank to high heaven and was bigger than the usual ferrets. I loved Jinx and I wrote a poem about him which I recited at school. Unfortunately, when The Twins were very young, they opened his cage, which was situated on the farmhouse terrace, and he escaped.

One time when The Twins were still babies, my mother opened the front door to find a ferret waiting on the threshold — it ran past her upstairs and into The Twins' little bedroom on the right, as if it had an appointment. It was soon added to our ferret gang.

On another occasion, while out ferreting, I came across a ferret walking through the woods. I thought I had found a new ferret but it turned out that the one I thought I was carrying had escaped from the box and I had, by chance, come across it.

When out ferreting, once you had recaptured the ferret, you had to make the decision to either give up on that warren or put the ferret down another hole. Generally, as it was time consuming to net a warren, you would send the ferret down again. Of course not all warrens are huge — some would be just a couple of holes.

If there was a rabbit down the hole then things could get very exciting very quickly.

One time I was in the wood at the very top of The Sloping Field when I heard what sounded like a galloping horse coming straight at me. I actually ducked down and rolled myself up into a ball, convinced I was about to be trampled. In fact it was a rabbit bolting underground.

When a rabbit came out it was usually travelling at

immense speed and it would burst into the net which would then close tight around it. Sometimes it pulled the peg out and the whole thing would fly out and you'd have to throw yourself at it.

Not infrequently a rabbit would bolt from the one hole we had missed and shoot away into the woods. Another common occurrence was that the rabbit would somehow slip past a badly set net and run away (followed by an argument about who netted that hole). Sometimes the rabbit appeared, saw us, and went back down the hole. For this reason we were very careful not to be visible from any hole, and we kept very quiet from the moment we arrived at a warren.

The worst outcome was if the ferret caught and killed a rabbit down the hole. If this happened you often heard the terrible screams coming from underground. It meant we were in for a very long wait. The ferret would kill the rabbit, gorge itself on it, and then have a sleep. This is why 'proper' ferreters have tracking collars on their ferrets and take digging equipment. Although we did eventually get a tracker we never managed to make it work.

If the ferret ate a rabbit it would often be completely pink with blood when it finally made an appearance.

When we did catch a rabbit the sense of triumph was overwhelming — we would be ecstatic. It was a feeling that was entirely instinctive and connected us with countless thousands of generations of hunting ancestors. Absurdly, in the early days, Rupert and I would get a stick and suspend the body of the rabbit from it by its fore and hind legs, as though it was a tiger or a wild boar. We knew how to do this correctly by cutting a hole in the animals tendons and threading one leg through the other. We would then carry it between us, the stick resting on our shoulders, all the way home. This was largely for the benefit of Mum who would describe us as 'the hunter home

CHAPTER 10

from the hill,' a quote from the poem *Requiem* by Robert Louis Stevenson.

We both learned not only to gut rabbits but also to skin them and prepare their pelts. We would do this by nailing the pelt to a board, furry side down. We would remove all the fat and flesh and cover it with a special salt. We would sometimes eat the meat ourselves or would feed it to the ferrets. The ferrets would also get the liver and kidney. On one occasion I made a near-perfect rabbit jelly which was spoiled only by the fact that a single rabbit poo, which I had missed while preparing the animal, was suspended within the jelly at the top, for all to see. Nobody would touch it.

'Hunters home from the hill' Adam (left) and Rupert

The most common outcome when we went ferreting, however, was that we caught nothing. Just occasionally, we would catch two. I think there may have been occasions when we caught three but my chief memory is of coming home with frozen feet and nothing else. I learned not to put my feet up against a radiator as this would cause absolute agony.

One skill I got from all that ferreting is the ability to gut and butcher any animal. On one occasion a man came to the farmhouse door and told Mum and I, with great sadness, that one of our deer had been killed on the road at Castle Hill. Mum and I looked at each other. We did not keep deer and it was clearly just a wild animal, but we thanked the man and went and collected the fresh kill. I strung it up by the hind legs on a tree and opened it up exactly as I would a rabbit. The meat was spectacular and lasted for months — but my abiding memory is of the colossal quantity of guts that I had to dispose of. There were three buckets of them.

We had a second hand heavy Brazilian-made side-by-side shotgun at Badsell and our other 'blood sport' was rough shooting. I would often walk around the farm with this heavy gun but I very seldom got close enough to anything, although I once shot a pigeon in flight which remains my 'best shot ever'. I would never shoot a wild pigeon today.

What we mainly used the gun for was lamping rabbits. We had an old van that was no longer 'street legal' and we cut a hole in the top and fixed a lamp up to the vehicle's battery. The shooter would stand with their head and shoulders poking out the top while the driver shot around the edges of the fields, screeching to a halt whenever a rabbit appeared. In most cases the rabbit was transfixed by the vehicles lights making it an easy target. Later I would go shooting on the Honda three wheeler motorbike, holding the loaded gun under my arm as I shot around the fields at crazy speeds.

We did not know it at the time but, in the early days at Badsell, Brian Wiseman was also hunting on the farm, though

CHAPTER 10

surreptitiously with a friend of his called Martin Butchers. Martin lived in Pembury and was a practiced 'countryman'. They used to snare foxes and sell them to a man in Horsmonden who bought them for their pelts. We too tried setting snares but it is a fine art and I don't recall ever catching anything.

Adam (left) and John Rogers, in the farmhouse kitchen after a rabbit shoot

At the age of about eight I was presented with a dog fox cub which a local farmer had found by a road. Nowadays anyone finding what appears to be an abandoned cub, or indeed any young animal, is advised to leave it as the chances are the parent is nearby — but I was not aware of this at the time.

It was of course absolutely beautiful, incredibly cute and completely wild. I felt like I was being presented with the most valuable jewel in the world.

Unusually I never gave the cub a name and this seems strange to me now — but I think the reason was that it always remained wild, despite my handling it a great deal. In fact he used to bite me every time I picked him up, sometimes quite hard and often drawing blood, particularly after he grew to full size which he did very quickly on its diet of dog food.

The fox never tamed at all and was as scared and aggressive on the last day as on the day I was presented with him. He used to pace back and forth in its large enclosure which took up the whole of one end of the pet shed. Once I was looking after him I didn't feel it was fair to let him go at least until he was strong enough to fend for himself.

When I did come to release him I was aware that he was unlikely to survive. He was never happy in captivity but the thought of humanely killing him was unthinkable and so I decided to let him take his chances.

I carried him up to the middle of the Park Field and let him go — expecting him to do what it had always appeared to want to do — which was to run as fast as it could to get away from me.

He did start to walk away but then he stopped and looked back at me. I had brought dog food and, for the first and only time, he walked up to me and ate out of my hand.

Having filled his belly he then headed towards the nearest cover. He glanced back at me once more, then he was gone. I never saw him again.

After that I was a bit obsessed with foxes and I still think of them as my favourite animal. These days I sometimes catch the distinctive scent of a fox when I am out walking in the countryside. It instantly reminds me of my pet fox.

At the age of 12 I wrote and recited a poem about a fox for the annual poetry contest at school. The previous year my poem had been about my polecat, Jinx, but this time I told the tale of a fox that escaped the hunt to live another day. I was awarded the prize for poetry recitation, in the sub category of 'self penned poems,' despite a long awkward pause when I temporarily forgot the last line. It meant that, for the only time in my whole school career, I got to walk up and accept a prize at the end of year prize giving.

CHAPTER 10

Adam with his fox, just before release

For the rest of my childhood, in spring and summer, I often used to rise at about 5 A.M. and go for a walk around the farm. Every time I did this I would see a fox and it always gave me a thrill. Sometimes the fox would not see me. At dawn, particularly away from roads and houses, foxes largely have the world to themselves and they are less wary. I would step closer and closer, sometimes coming within just a few feet before it would suddenly spy me and scarper.

The biggest thrill came on a foggy summer morning when I came across a fox chasing a rabbit in the field below The Pear Orchard. I might as well have been watching a lion trying to bring down a gazelle on the Serengeti. The rabbit was darting back and forth and the pair of them would disappear into the fog and then reemerge. To me it was intensely beautiful and dramatic thing to witness.

I would see all sorts of things on those walks and I once

came across a muntjac deer in the End Field. At the time I didn't know what it was and as it scarpered away it bounced up and down, all four legs held straight. It was the most bizarre thing I had ever seen and I breathlessly described it to Mum on my return to the house. She was knowledgeable about wildlife and knew what it was immediately — and shared my excitement.

The rarest thing we ever saw on the farm was probably a water rail although it was rare only in that it was clearly lost. Water rails are wetland wading birds and there were no reed beds at Badsell.

Sadly we only became aware that we had a water rail on the farm when the cat brought it in.

The bird was incredibly exotic to us and we were horrified to see that the cat was treating it as just another small animal to toy with before delivering the fatal bite. We took it to the vets in Paddock Wood where it was identified, sewn up, and handed back to us for post-operative care. We kept it in a box during its recovery and eventually released it but we did not particularly rate its chances and we never quite looked at the cat the same way again.

Although there were kingfishers living along the Tudely Brook we almost never saw them. In fact we only confirmed they were there when local farmer, Barney Wise, set up a camera by the stream with a device that triggered the shutter when a bird landed on it.

The most common bird on the farm were sparrows many of which lived in a noisy high rise 'apartment' consisting of a giant climbing bush affixed to the side of the back of the oast house, facing the farmhouse terrace. There must have been hundreds of nests in that bush and there was often a huge racket as the thousands of sparrows all cheeped away. Rupert and I used to go around shooting them at night with an air rifle as some would

CHAPTER 10

sleep in the barns and could be spotted with torches. We regarded sparrows as disposable and the same farmer who photographed the kingfisher, Barney Wise, once told me he had shot fifty with a single blast of his shotgun. He put down a line of corn and fired from his driving seat through the passenger window. He told me he forgot to open the passenger window which exploded.

CHAPTER 11
THE PERFECT VENUE

The heart of our social life at Badsell was the 'hunting lodge' room in the farmhouse where we sat around a large polished mahogany dining table eating, telling stories, drinking huge quantities of cheap wine, pitching our wits against each other and laughing uproariously, the whole scene reflected in a huge elaborately framed floor to ceiling mirror.

My mother was incapable of saying, "If I had known you were going to be here, I would have invited you to join us." Instead, to any guest who happened to drop by, she would say, "Have supper with us - there's plenty of food." If there wasn't enough she would just boil a load more pasta or rice or she would say, 'FHB' which stood for 'family hold back' — meaning we took smaller portions.

In reality there was always enough and it was always good. A favourite meal was chicken thighs sizzling away in a juice made of tomatoes, onions, garlic and herbs, or a massive spaghetti Bolognese. She was adept at making curries too, a legacy of her origins as a child of the 'Raj'. She made her own dhal from scratch, fried stacks of popadoms and always made sure there was mango chutney. She taught me that even if you

CHAPTER 11

overcook the rice you can 'revive' it by suspending it on a sieve over boiling water. Another speciality of Mum's was roast pheasant, a brace of which were occasionally left by one of our shooting friends and left to hang outside the back door. She would pluck them, seated on the low wall by the stream outside the back door, and served them with fried breadcrumbs, cranberry sauce, roast potatoes, sprouts, red cabbage, bread sauce and a rich gravy.

After the meal all smokers lit up, which eventually meant the entire family and most of our guests. The quantity of smoke this produced can be imagined.

When I was 17 my father came up to my room and said, "If you smoke, don't do it up here — you can smoke with us downstairs." That very evening I had my first cigarette in front of my parents while we were watching TV. Almost immediately after I lit up, a public service advert came on featuring Superman telling kids not to smoke because it would kill them. I felt overwhelming embarrassment but it did not put me off. Thank God I managed to quit before I was twenty-one.

Another dinner in the heart of the farmhouse. (From centre clockwise: John Rogers, Sam Thornely, Elizabeth Kirkor Rogers, Nick Lutter, John, Celia, Anto and Ruth Thornely, Emma)

As a family we loved to tell stories and laugh. Laughter was important, in fact it was the main reason for living. One of the advantages of this was that no disaster was ever really a disaster — because later, in the telling, it could be made amusing. 'Funny in a fortnight' was the family motto. It was only later in life that I discovered that some people don't live like this at all. They regard disasters as bad things to be avoided and, if they do occur, to be hushed up entirely — or only spoken about in a serious way with the intention of avoiding a repetition.

Only recently have a realised that Badsell was, in some ways, a recreation of the atmosphere and life that Mum had lived during a magical period of her childhood living at Peynetts in Goudhurst. Here her mother Ruth had kept a very 'open house', with a busy social scene which itself was probably inspired by the lifestyle she had enjoyed with husband Frank in Bombay. At Peynetts Ruth was very much the matriarch and even had what her son Nick refers to as 'stepdaughters'. These were two girls, Carolyn Coleman and Jenny Howard, who had lost their mothers, and so they found a warm welcome in the Thornely household. Carolyn remained one of Mum's dearest friends throughout her life.

The big event at Peynetts was the Christmas dance. Ruth insisted all her children took dancing lessons and the music of Victor Sylvester and Joe loss would be played on a wind up gramophone. Nick remembers his cousin Tim Barnes attending dressed up as a lady of the Middle Ages. Tim was sitting, somewhat ignored, when Frank Thornely went up and asked 'her' to dance, saying afterwards 'I felt sorry for her'.

That spirit of fun and dressing up persisted at Badsell. On her fiftieth birthday Mum requested that, instead of gifts, we all perform a show. Her brothers Nick and Anto sang a song, Nan read a Kipling poem, and Rupert did a magic trick (with his wife Sam acting as his glamorous assistant). Dad recited 'The Green

CHAPTER 11

Eye of the Yellow God' by J Milton Hayes (substituting the word 'Paddock Wood' for 'Khatmandu'), John Rogers dressed up as a Yukon beaver hunter and recited 'The Cremation of Sam McGee' by Robert Service, and my sister Emma sang 'Summertime' accompanied on the piano by Jason Piette. I created a comic skit in which I played Mum as distracted and overworked. In the story a monster kept trying to kill her but because she was dealing with endless crises on the farm he never got a look in. John and Charles played themselves having an endless series of accidents, the most serious of which was on The Honda three-wheeler.

Mum was essentially a creative person. Although she wanted the house to be tidy she would rather paint a picture, make a sculpture, weed a flower bed, visit an art gallery, catch up with someone over a coffee, in fact do almost anything other than housework. As a child I recall her making a beautiful sculpture of one of her horses out of wire and plaster of Paris. Having trained in Paris just after the war she was a very accomplished artist.

The farmhouse was the kind of house where you could never find a pair of scissors unless you could work out who used them last and where they had used them. The most chaotic room of all was a little tool room off the downstairs corridor. It was often barely possible to enter it. Even Mum's little office by the 'hunting lodge' room, was chaotic, even though this was the business centre for the farm, where the check books were kept and the farm accounts were kept.

The person who tried to help get us organised was Mum's dearest friend Elizabeth Kirkor Rogers who came up with various schemes to get the place more organised, including creating 'pigeon holes' for all of us in the kitchen. This was a simple system of shelves where all of our mail could be organised and any other pieces of paper or items could be placed. The pigeon holes did work, although all her other schemes fell by the wayside due to our refusal to cooperate.

The office in the farmhouse (Photo: Elizabeth Kirkor Rogers)

One day Mum was cooking a meal in the kitchen and she asked Lizzie to lay the table in the dining room. She went to the cutlery drawer which was always filled with an assortment of antique silver and ivory handled cutlery. She was pulling out knives, forks and spoons when she came across a strange metal gadget, with metal circles and a kind of a plunger. She asked Mum what it was and she replied "Oh, that's for castrating the goats."

But for all the chaos there was one item that we all knew had to be returned to its proper place - Mum's secateurs. If they went missing she would be on the warpath. Probably Mum's greatest passion of all was gardening and she never lost a sense of wonder about the miracle of seeds sprouting.

At Badsell she was so busy that she was not able to indulge her love of gardening as much as she would have liked, yet she did spend many hours digging and weeding the various flower beds and the farmhouse garden was filled with colour in spring and summer. The edges of the terrace were planted with a row of lavender, within which, as children, we discovered cuckoo spit, the clusters of foam within which lives the froghopper. In

CHAPTER 11

this same bed there was always a thick cluster of parsley which never seemed to run out. On the other side of the terrace Mum planted a honeysuckle and she taught us to snap off a flower then pinch its base and pull out a length of 'string,' on the end of which was a perfect drop of delicious nectar.

At the age of nearly seventy, after we had left Badsell, Mum was selected from 40,000 applicants by Diarmuid Gavin to be trained as a Garden Designer for a BBC programme called Diarmuid Gavin's Garden School. With the eight other selected participants she went through an intense training at the Royal Horticultural Society's headquarters at RHS Wisley. Part of the course required them to dig, plant and tend their own vegetable patch and Mum was always up first, and digging away, while several of the other candidates (the oldest of whom was half her age) suffered pulled muscles and back injuries. One of the other contestants, Catherine Lawlor, wrote afterwards: "It was such a pleasure to spend time with her. She cooked for us and cared for us and was loads of fun to be with. We went out drawing together and she taught me how to paint with watercolours." When Diarmuid Gavin heard that Mum had died he wrote, "Celia was an inspiration, elegant, fun, innovative...always with a twinkle in her eye. I loved her...we all loved her."

Being part of this TV show was something of a highlight of Mum's life, it was a moment when she really got to shine and it lead to her having a variety of sweet pea (her favourite flower) named after her. Following her appearance on this show, at an age when many people have long retired, Mum began a new career as a garden designer and had many very satisfied clients. She loved the work and found it difficult to charge money for something that gave her so much pleasure. She may have inherited her love of gardening - and flowers in particular - from her father Frank, although for him this interest proved disastrous.

Celia with Diarmuid Gavin and a cake created by
Unwins to celebrate the launch of Sweet Pea Celia,
the flower named after her.

While the family were living in Goudhurst he set up a nursery business in Marden, growing orchids. He had a business partner who drove a flashy green 1938, 3.5 litre Jaguar. This partner absconded with the company's finances or in some way mismanaged things. The business went bust and the consequences were devastating. Frank was forced to sell their beloved Paynetts and they had to move to a flat in Hungershall Park, Tunbridge Wells. The only up side, according Mum's brother Nick, was that they inherited the car. "My beautiful mother, driving up to our prep school in this fantastic Jaguar, it was a terrific morale raiser", says Nick today, but he also believes that Ruth never forgave her husband for risking, and losing, their idyllic life at Peynetts.

The absolute antithesis of our family attitude at Badsell, something so alien to us that it was like a sort of kryptonite, was the 'round robin' letter that some families would innocently send us at Christmas.

You might think that we would read these things out loudly and scornfully, making nasty remarks about the unbearable showing off about their children's success in gaining a place at Oxford, or their wonderful trip to the Caribbean - but the truth was we didn't read them at all — or at least only Mum did, being

CHAPTER 11

the least cynical amongst us. They were regarded by the rest of us as the most extreme example imaginable of bottled boredom. We occasionally talked of doing a comic one, in which we would describe all the disasters that had befallen us over the year and the disgraceful things we had done, but we never got around to it.

At dinner we loved to exchange stories but we also played games, for example my father might ask us to name a snake beginning with 'A'. He would then work his way through the alphabet.

A favourite game was 'The Book Game'. This involved choosing a book at random from one of the many shelves dotted about the house (we owned hundreds of books). The 'referee' would then read out the title and the name of the author and everyone would write down what they believed was a convincing first line from the book. The referee then read out all these first lines, with the real one mixed in, and we voted on which we believed was the real one. Points were awarded for choosing the correct one, or if your own fake one was selected by another contestant (you could not vote for your own!). The game sounds complex and pretentious but it works because it is often surprisingly difficult to tell which is the real first line, and you get hilariously bad or comic first lines. The Twins started joining in this game when they were still quite young and on one occasion someone chose the book 'Little Women' by Louisa May Alcott. Charles wrote as his first line: "Women come in three sizes: small, medium and large". Another time the book chosen was a historical romance titled "Royal Flush" by Margaret Irwin. One of the entries was read out by Dad: "I awoke to the sound of gunfire, the privy was to be used that day". In fact he had misread someone's bad handwriting and it read: "I awoke to the sound of gunfire, the prince was to be wed that day."

GOODBYE BADSELL

Farmhouse terrace with the young honeysuckle plant climbing up the post. (Left to right: Unknown, Rupert, Celia, John Rogers, Adam, Roland Rogers, Photo: Elizabeth Kirkor Rogers).

As the teen years began we started to make maximum use of the amazing place that we lived. Our first parties were held in the two kilns in the large oast house. Immediately above them were slatted ceilings on which the hops had once been laid out. We discovered that if we suspended a lightbulb in the 'reek' above, and swung it, the shadows of the floor slats created an awesome lighting effect below. It felt like the whole floor was swinging wildly back and forth.

We decided this would make a great disco light — but of course it just made everyone feel seasick and had to be switched off.

To get the rooms ready we had to clear a whole load of 'junk' out that my parents had piled up. This included old fashioned heavy wooden skis and ski boots which seemed positively Victorian to us but where in fact just a few years old. More interestingly there were items from my grandfather Frank Thornely's time in the First World War. This included a camp bed which would later find its way up to the 'Hut in the Woods'. There was also his helmet, water bottle, leather bags, medical paraphernalia (including a stretcher) and what I loved most: a collection of The Bystander Magazine, full of cartoons about life on the front lines. One was the famous Bruce Bairnsfather cartoon, part of his 'Fragments from France' series, depicting two miserable British soldiers in a shell hole, with explosions going off all around them and one saying, 'Well, if you knows of a better 'ole, go to it".

The large space above what would one day be the gift shop played host to Rupert's 12th birthday party which was attended by about thirty children with the sexes split equally. He came up with the theme for the party himself and it was 'Kissing Competition'. He himself had the job of judging all the girls and his girlfriend, Stephanie Webb, judged the boys. They only had one record to play which was The Beatles 'Please Please Me' which was played over and over again. Marks were awarded out of ten for kissing and at the end, the results were that Rupert won "Best Boy kisser" and Stephanie, his girlfriend, won "Best Girl Kisser."

In our teen years, we woke up to the potential of the big Atcost barn for organising raves. By then it had been converted into a play barn. It had been clad in wood and given a little entrance area and a large minstrels gallery reached by a flight of stairs. There was also a slide running from the minstrel's gallery to the floor of the main play area where toy equipment, including an inflatable 'ball pond' was laid out.

Of course for the raves all this had to be cleared away. The raves were generally very popular and would go on until late on a Saturday night. This was the 1990s, the time of 'illegal rave' culture when people would meet up at the World of Leather in South East London. There they would exchange information about where that night's raves were being held. Word about the 'Badsell' raves would enter the grapevine and we would get all sorts arriving. John remembers coaches turning up. In fact a lot of the promotion of the raves was done by Emma, using the resources available to her at her office in Soho. She was working at the time in advertising.

She would do big mail outs using the company's franking machine.

The Big Barn after conversion to a playbarn

On the nights themselves Emma would stand at the end of the drive with The Twins and our dog Jessie, checking tickets, taking money and generally being 'security'.

My Dad knew that the raves were bringing in money but he also knew that the constant 'thud thud' of loud music would lead to problems, especially after the government clamped down on illegal raves.

On one occasion, when he had repeatedly tried to get the DJ to turn the music down, he ended up standing at the decks, in his dressing gown, up on the minstrel's gallery, holding the volume down with his hand while the entire heaving crowd chanted at him: "*Wanker, wanker wanker.*"

After extracting the sincerest of promises from the DJ that he would keep the volume down, Dad went back to the farmhouse and back upstairs to bed but as his head hit the pillow the music was again turned up full blast. The next time he

CHAPTER 11

appeared he brought a hammer with him and he threatened to destroy the equipment there and then, in front of everyone.

One bizarre feature of the raves was that Jessie, the giant black dog, used to love joining in. Her favourite place to stand was right by the huge speakers. Presumably she wanted to get the full effect of the bass. Possibly she was deaf following the incident where Mum shot her with the twelve bore after she savaged the Wensleydale Ram.

The neighbours who lived on Crittenden Lane near the end of the drive always complained about the noise of the raves, despite being a quarter of a mile away, and the Police were always called.

We hated the police coming because pretty much everything we were doing was illegal. We would claim it was a private party, usually saying that we were celebrating Emma's birthday. We would even try and have an element of fancy dress to make it look less like a public ticketed event, which it clearly wasn't. We also had to pretend that we were not selling alcohol, which we clearly were. We didn't have a leg to stand on so we would stop the music and try desperately to get rid of hundreds of irate people. John remembers his bike being stolen from the yard then repeatedly run over on the drive, probably an act of frustration by someone who had been high on ecstasy, trancing out to The Shamen, only to have their state of bliss interrupted by an angry man in a dressing gown, waving a hammer, followed by an unwelcome appearance by the Old Bill.

Things were always a bit messy the next day. The whole place had to be cleaned up, hundred of cigarette butts picked up and the play barn turned back into a toddler's paradise. To add to the complications we would always have a lot of friends to stay who would be sleeping on every bed and sofa and anywhere else they could find. They would then emerge late morning, with hangovers, wanting full fry ups in the café.

GOODBYE BADSELL

The combination of endless parties and running a petting zoo for the public created endless little incidents. Gail Belton remembers that for a while The Twins moved into a caravan at the far side of the pet area near the pig sties. On a Sunday morning she would arrive early to feed the animals aware that The Twins and their friends would all be sleeping off a heavy night. She would open the lid of an old freezer that was used to store the pig food and the sound would set the pigs off screaming for their breakfast — one of the loudest, most piercing and annoying sounds in nature. She would then wander around feeding all the other animals first, smiling to herself.

On one occasion, the day after a party, a lot of our friends were gathered on the grass by the stream in front of the farm- house. Unwisely some of them started messing about on the Honda three- wheeler motorbike.

When people use a three wheeler motorbike for the first time they often lean the wrong way when they come to turn their first corner. The first time Rupert got on ours he drove straight into the stream and the bike landed on top of him. On another occasion I went for a walk around the farm and by chance I came across Charles, aged about seven years old, trapped underneath the bike. I lifted it off him and I remember he stood very nonchalant with a hand in his pocket, discussing the accident.

John also liked using the bike when he was arguably too small and on one occasion he was shooting at immense speed down the field behind the stables. He took off at the top of the slope that takes you down to the driveway. In mid air he realised he was on a collision course with a Renault 5 filled with old ladies.

In slow motion he saw the old biddies smile at his cute little boy face, then look horrified as they realised he was on a powerful machine that was about to smash into them. He ripped the bonnet clean off their car.

I used to love tearing around the borders of the farm on that bike and because I did it so often I became adept at covering the distance in just a few minutes. On one occasion I did this with John on the back, when he was quite small. There was a point where I went through the stream by 'the fallen log' that goes from the Sewer Field into the woods by the Sloping Field. I was tearing up the steep slope on the far side of the stream when I realised it was too steep and we were about to go over backwards. This was bad news as the weight of the bike and myself was about to land on John. At the crucial moment John leaned abruptly forwards, changing the centre of gravity, and we were back on our way. It is hard to fit all the near-deaths on the Honda three wheeler into one book but perhaps I can squeeze another one in here. Graham Creswell, who these days is the Twin's business partner in LPM Bohemia, The Tent Company, managed to crash into an old yew tree that once stood in the middle of the lawn in front of the farmhouse, afterwards careering into my godfather Patrick Mercheson's car.

Getting back to the *main* Honda three-wheeler incident, on the morning after the party in question a group of our friends were playing about on the vehicle when the driver, Ben Musgrave, hit a telegraph pole at speed.

Ben, the brother of Rupert's then girlfriend (and later wife) hit his head on the telegraph pole so hard that he was knocked unconscious and all the phones on the farm were immediately disconnected. This was before mobile phones, so the farm was now cut off from the outside world.

While Samantha stayed with her brother, who was initially completely out cold with his eyes still wide open, a posse was sent down the drive to the nearest house to ask if they could call for an ambulance.

Of course this house contained the very people who had shut down the rave the night before and they were in a state of rage about their disturbed night and in no mood to cooperate with a delegation from the very farm which was the source of their torment. When the posse arrived they point blank refused to let anyone in to use the telephone.

Luckily, when the situation was explained, they did agree to call the ambulance.

Rowley Kirby on the Honda three-wheeler with John and Charles during Emma's wedding celebrations

When Ben regained consciousness on the way to the hospital he noticed that the nurse tending to him was rather attractive. His first words were, "Hello, what's your name?"

Having hungover characters knocking about on Sunday was very much par for the course at Badsell. On one occasion a poetic friend called Locket Somerville came to an event dressed as Oscar Wilde. He maintained the character of Oscar throughout the weekend and continued the performance on Monday morning on the commuter train back to London, with Dad seated opposite him in the carriage.

CHAPTER 11

Another time my father organised an elaborate launch for his new butterfly house which had been built inside the pet area at one end of the chicken barn.

At that time Dad was rubbing shoulders with the odd celebrity in his work heading up the Think British Campaign, which was designed to get people to buy British goods (our friend John Rogers, who is American, worked for him for a while and the family joke was that he was ordering people, in his American accent, to "think British y'all!"). Dad had become friendly with a married couple called Michael Denison and Dulcie Grey, both British film stars of the silver screen. He invited them to come for the grand opening of the butterfly house and, as if such stellar names were not enough, he also got Edward Kelsey, Joe Grundy in the long-running Radio 4, agriculturally-themed drama The Archers. Grundy was there to launch a 'nature trail'.

A good deal of thought had gone into the creation of the butterfly house. Dad had found a fellow lepidopterist in Nigel Hodges from Tatlingbury Farm at Five Oak Green and together they visited Kew Gardens to get ideas on what 'exotics' to plant. This had then partly partly dictated which species to order up from the various live butterfly and moth catalogues.

The launch event involved two separate mishaps. One occurred during Dad's speech on the terrace of the farmhouse during which he very clearly referred to Dulcie Grey as 'Dulcie Waters'. I was not sure why he did this at the time but assumed it was an obscure joke and I laughed loudly to support my father. Everyone else remained silent and in fact it was simply a cock up — and like all cock ups it must therefore be recorded here for posterity.

The other notable happening occurred in the butterfly house. About mid morning my sister Emma looked out of the front door of the farmhouse and saw that her friend Charles

Fontaine, a French restauranteur, was getting into his car. She walked over and asked him why he was leaving.

"I have to go," he replied in his heavy French accent, *"because I trod on ze moeth"*

Nigel Hodges, Dulcie Gray and Michael Denison during the opening of the butterfly house.

It turned out that during the other important part of the day's events — the official opening of the butterfly house by Michael Dennison and Dulcie Grey, there had been great excitement because, as chance would have it, one of the chrysalises that Dad had purchased by mail order had been completing the long and drawn out business of hatching.

It has been said since that this moth was the most magnificent of all — the Atlas moth — but this might be an exaggeration. Whatever the truth, all the assembled guests, the two celebrities, my father, his assistant in the 'moth and butterfly department (Nigel Hodges), and various members of the public and hung-over remnants from the night before, had been watching this moth when, to everyone's delight and amazement, it released its grip on the branch it had been drying on and alighted on the floor, producing a gasp of wonder.

At that moment Charles Fontaine had wandered into the Butterfly House, not even aware that a butterfly house was

CHAPTER 11

being launched, but just searching for a fry up to ease his hangover.

He trod on the moth with his great big designer-shoe-clad foot, and squashed it.

The big Atcost barn was where we held any big parties such as my sister's wedding banquet. To decorate it I cut tall hazel saplings and affixed them all around the inside walls, creating the sense that you were eating in a woodland glade — well that was the intention but actually they were rather thin, the foliage a little sparse, so it was really just a slight distraction from the brutal concrete and steel. Emma's wedding was a great occasion, attended by a huge number of people, and was the first recorded incident of one of The Twins, (Charles) getting drunk. Mid afternoon I heard him groaning upstairs in the farmhouse in 'Ben's Loo'.

One year a friend of my brother's called James Purefoy, a successful actor, decided to have his 30th birthday party in the barn.

James liked to do things with style. He selected the 'Wild West' as his theme and we created a wild west bar, had a lot of bales of hay and generally threw a lot of gingham at the event. There was a live band with a 'caller' organising the dancing and at one point James and a professional stuntman had a choreographed barroom brawl.

A big issue with a party like that was — where was everyone going to sleep? James himself, who at the time was going out with Janet McTeer (also a successful actor who has since garnered two Oscar nominations), had paid an extra £75 to have my brother Rupert's bedroom at the top of the house. The room was prepared specially and James enjoyed himself all the more knowing that he had a big comfy bed awaiting him and Janet.

My father was very taken with the fact that someone had paid the princely sum of £75 for Rupert's bedroom and at some point in the evening he went up to check that everything was prepared. To his horror he found that the door had become jammed shut. He worked himself up into a hell of a sweat trying to get it open and eventually came up with the idea of applying a screwdriver to the problem. After a great deal of straining and swearing he managed to take the door off its hinges.

Pleased with himself he went back to join the party and seeing James he went over to speak to him.

"All set for later?" he said to James who deftly took a large key from his pocket and held it up.

"I certainly am Simon," he said, "and I've got the key right here."

Saying nothing Dad headed back to the farmhouse, up the stairs to the third floor and rehung the door. It had never occurred to him that the door might have a working lock.

Once the petting zoo and cafe were up and running Badsell became a very popular place for children to hold their birthday parties but before that we had memorable birthday parties of our own.

In 1976 a remake of King Kong was made ("The most exciting motion picture event of all time!") and the whole family went along to the cinema at the top of Mount Pleasant in Tunbridge Wells. We all loved the film but it seemed to delight my Dad in particular. He was so inspired that when it came to planning Rupert's 12th birthday party in November of that year he decided that there had to be a 'gorilla hunt'.

He hired himself a gorilla costume and on one of those crisp clear November days he set off to run around the farm. After a suitable pause, a small hoard of boys were allowed set off in pursuit.

Something primal took over and we were all in seventh heaven — feeling like we were chasing the ultimate beast. As a birthday activity it had everything — we burned off energy, there was a sense of danger, and our atavistic hunting instincts were awakened. Dad, who had not really thought through what the rules were, just ran, with a growing sense of unease. What would happen if the gang of boys caught him? But he was fairly fit and managed to get most of the way around the farm. Finally, however, he was brought down by a Nigerian boy called Kenny Odogwu, a brilliant athlete who was a boarder at Holmewood House School.

Rupert's birthday gorilla hunt (left to right: Adam, Emma, Simon (in gorilla suit), Rupert, Timothy Robbins, Simon Westen, Kenny Odogwu, Steven Wiseman

I remember I coveted the prize which Kenny was awarded — a rubber King Kong toy which seemed to me to be the best thing in the world.

Years later, when John and Charles were old enough, we had more gorilla hunts. Rupert donned the outfit for one. Graham Cresswell remembers being absolutely terrified when he spied a gorilla speeding towards him on the Honda three wheeler, like something out of Planet of the Apes. Another year myself and my friend Spencer Ewen both got to don gorilla suits. At one point we became exhausted. These were our 'partying years' when we smoked and drank excessively and were horribly unfit. We took refuge in Solly's Wood half way up the sloping field. As we stood recovering a boy appeared. He had somehow got away from the pack and had stumbled on the two panting gorillas by chance. It seemed a pitiable ending to a gorilla hunt and Spencer and I spontaneously decided we were not to be taken so easily. We ran at him roaring and he shrank into the ground.

For another of the twin's birthdays I created a quiz with questions written on cards that were secreted around the general area of the sewer field. There were things like 'is the current James Bond Film Called:'

1. Never Say Never Again
2. Never Say either 'Never' or 'Ever' or any of the following: 'Either', 'Or', 'Neither', 'Always' or 'Whatever'"
3. The Awful Smell

Another question showed a photograph of a white frizzle hen and the question was: Is this Hen

1. Meant to look like this or
2. It has been through a washing machine.

The questions were meant to be funny but of course there was a right or wrong answer. I remember seeing one boy, his little face contorted with intense concentration as he tried to interpret the nonsense.

The boys got their own back though. After the quiz we

CHAPTER 11

played a giant game of British Bulldogs on the grass field between the Sewer Field and the stream. Being bigger than the boys I was the last man standing and feeling rather pleased with myself. I set off to try and cross the field again, with everyone now trying to bring me down. It looked as though I was going to make it too, which felt like an achievement, when I found myself running towards a boy who, I suddenly realised, was armed with a rock. He threw it and caught me directly in the balls. I was brought down like a felled ox and writhed about in the grass in agony, the laughter of about twenty boys ringing in my ears.

Later when they were teenagers, the boys began organising their own parties for their birthdays which fall in October. One, in the Atcost Barn when they were probably 16, was held in temperatures of about minus 10. In an attempt to heat it they set up a space heater which blasted out hot air. It made no impression on the temperature and girls in their skimpy outfits were reduced to sitting as close to this thing as they could, burning themselves on one side while the body parts facing away from the heater froze.

Badsell was a natural place to hold events because there was ample space. Parking was only ever a problem when the ground was wet, which of course it often was. Then Mum would despair because the great ruts left by stuck vehicles would take years and years to get rid of. "Oh God - the land!" she would cry.

Every year at Badsell we held a Guy Fawkes Night around November the 5th and we would always build a huge bonfire. The event was always extremely well attended by families with small children, possibly because it was felt likely that it would be a 'small-child friendly' event, due to the fact that we had a petting zoo. When The Twins were only around 12 years old they were put in charge of actually lighting the fireworks.

Charles set up what he calls a large 'mortar' in the soft earth. He then dropped a thing like a coconut into the open end after lighting its fuse. The thing apparently went off underground. There was no flash in the sky or any spectacle - just a very loud deep boom that hit you in the chest. As Charles puts it "there was a slight pause then hundreds of children all burst into tears at once". He recalls feeling "very satisfied" with this result and he immediately continued, with John, to set up the next explosion.

A lot of the events that took place such as the dog shows, terrier racing, hunter trials and clay shoots, were organised by other people.

One such event was the Andean Day which was organised by Jessica Gorst-Williams, a Daily Telegraph journalist who had some connection with South America. This event took place at the beginning of the 1990's when I was living in New York and I only heard about it afterwards. It was a celebration of the shared culture of the Andean States and seems to have been a huge piss up due to the availability of Pisco Sours, the Peruvian cocktail.

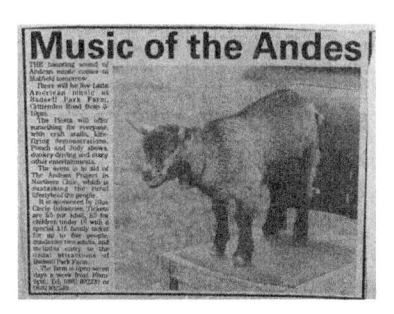

For some reason Cosmo Fry had a stall demonstrating the game Perudo. The Twins claim there was an ugly scene in the farmhouse where various ambassadors from the Andean States were gathered together for cocktails. Apparently bitter rivalries

CHAPTER 11

were exposed in heated exchanges. They also allege that one of the farm workers, William Mcinally, drunk on Pisco Sours, lost control of his moped and partially brought down the marquee while a little old lady, also the worst for wear, took out the red telephone box which stood on the front lawn, a legacy of Rupert's entrepreneurial endeavours in the field of sandblasting.

Not all the events we held at Badsell were an unmitigated success.

When it was announced that the Tour de France was coming through Kent I foolishly got caught up in the hype. The cyclists were due to go down Crittenden Lane and past the farm entrance and I attended some dreary meeting, organised by local government, that was meant to help businesses maximise the benefits. Of course when it came to it, Crittenden Lane was shut so no customers could actually reach the farm.

One day someone had the idea of going large on Mothering Sunday. At this point we had brought in outside caterers at the suggestion of a business consultant.

Having gone into partnership with these caterers we were trying to take things up a notch in the café. So the idea was to offer a full Sunday roast and, crucially (and unusually) people could book in advance for Mothering Sunday.

Now most people have a mother and it is a fact that anywhere that can rustle up a half decent lunch tends to be booked up on the big day. I recall returning from somewhere and I met Mum on the front porch of the farmhouse as I was going in. She told me: "We have over a hundred bookings for Mothering Sunday." Rather than tell her I thought this sounded like a disaster in the making, I turned on my heels and went back to my car. It was my pantomime way of saying "this is going to be a catastrophe and I want nothing to do with it." She laughed.

On the day a hundred or so people did indeed turn up -

with their mothers and other guests - as might be expected. After all they had booked.

The problem was the caterers had never dealt with such numbers before. I'm not sure if they had ever even seen so many people in one place. They didn't really have the equipment or the skills required to cook so many roasts and they couldn't cope.

Everyone got roped into helping but the 'helpers' included people like Dad who was simply not made to work in the service industry. At one point he went out into the garden and placed a tray of drinks on the grass and wandered away. The pressure had become too much, he could not for the life of him think who the drinks were for, and he decided instead to make them an offering to the gods.

Customers had to wait hours for their food. My sister Emma remembers asking someone if they wanted desert and they replied "I think I'll have to cancel work tomorrow if I'm having desert."

Afterwards there was a post-mortem in the big drawing room in the farmhouse. The two men from the catering company were sitting there with my parents and the chef. The idea was to identify what had gone wrong and insure that it never happened again. But the Chef was so exhausted he was just flopped over at the waist in his chair, his head dangling down between his knees. He couldn't speak.

We needed to come up with ideas for events at Badsell in order to attract a bigger crowd than the usual weekend visitors, which largely consisted of families with small children. When Rupert acquired an old fire engine this became the basis for an event we put on called the 'Big Fire Caper'. Someone else owned a multicoloured VW Beetle so the 'show' involved a bunch of 'thieves' turning up and committing some sort of heist. Somehow the fire engine was woven into the narrative. After-

CHAPTER 11

wards it became a permanent part of a play area after being made relatively safe for toddlers.

Sophie Denny promoting the Badsell Park Fayre in Maidstone

Another event that enjoyed mixed success was The Badsell Park Fayre. This was going to be a sort of medieval fair but although we spent weeks planning it, we failed to attract the huge crowds we had hoped for. I was heavily involved and did leafletting in Tonbridge and Maidstone dressed as a jester, with Sophie Denny who was dressed as a pig.

In Tonbridge I put the leaflets on the windscreens of about a hundred cars in a big car park near the station. This seemed to me to be a wonderfully efficient way of spreading the word but I was made to remove every single leaflet by a uniformed official upon whom my charm failed to work, even in my amusing costume. My knee started to hurt and I became the least jovial jester in history.

I designed a poster for the 'Fayre' and special T shirts which portrayed a rock band of pigs. Another one showed an escaped pig with the words 'Pig Out at Badsell!' These T-shirts remained unsold in the farm shop for years, their number gradually diminished through theft.

On the day of the Fayre my sister Emma presided over everything dressed as Maid Marion on her horse, Rosie. We had a sort of parade on the front lawn, with me providing my usual out-of-sync commentary due to the lack of a direct view of what was happening.

The highlight was the pig racing which caused huge excitement, with people even placing bets.

One mate, called Joel Bradley, had decided that The Badsell Park Fare was going to launch his new business selling framed Winnie the Pooh pictures - of which he sold not one. The only person who did well financially was a lady telling fortunes in a little tent on the front lawn. There was huge snaking queue outside her tent all day and long into the evening. I was very struck by how much faith people placed in her word. The next day one of the teenaged girls who worked in the gift shop told me that she had been told the exact date that she was going to conceive a child.

Pig racing at the Badsell Park Fayre

We had planned an evening party as well but when it came to it we sold almost no tickets and I remember having a big row with the manager of a brilliant Ska band called the Ja Penguins who, naturally enough, still wanted us to pay the full agreed fee even though they were just playing to us.

We did hold many evening parties as well - such as a medieval banquet, at which we roasted one of our own pigs. In preparation for this event John and I drove all the way to Wales

CHAPTER 11

to collect a job lot of Medieval goblets and other paraphernalia but when we got there, after driving for about seven hours, we discovered that it was a load of cheap garbage and we drove back empty handed.

Emma overseeing the Badsell Park Fayre in costume on Rosie

GOODBYE BADSELL

Rupert Preston, Samantha Musgrave and Poodle the dog welcomed visitors to Badsell Park fun day on Saturday

Rupert and his girlfriend Samantha in press coverage for the Badsell Park Fayre or 'Fun Day', 1992

CHAPTER 12
HORSES

ONE OF THE REASONS MY MOTHER WAS SO KEEN TO OWN land was that she was an accomplished and passionate horsewoman.

She had first encountered ponies as a very young child in India, a country she left at the age of 5. There had also been a pony at Porlock in Somerset where the family rented a country house immediately after the War. After a period in London the Thornely family started looking for somewhere to live in either Suffolk or Kent.

They eventually settled in Goudhurst in Kent, a village that Frank happened upon while touring the county. He declared it the most beautiful village he had ever seen and that he was going to live there. Here the Thornelys lived at a house called Paynetts, which had enough grounds for a grass tennis court (which Frank built) and a pony paddock where Shandy and Bracken lived. Mum's brother Nick described their time at Paynett's as the 'fairyland life', and horses were a big part of that. They hunted with the Ashford Valley and Eridge Hunts and went to Pony Club camps, although as Nick puts it 'Celia was by far the better rider, I went along on her coat tails'. If they went to a gymkhana they 'hacked' there, having no horse box. They became great friends with the Roberts family who lived in their ancestral seat of Glassenbury House - a breathtaking moated mansion. When they attended horsey events at Glassenbury they and their horses were put up for the night.

Celia on Oyster Bay (Photo: Elizabeth Kirkor Rogers)

At Badsell Mum's horse, Oyster Bay, was the first occupant of the stables. Dad rode Oyster Bay for a while until he got thrown in the Park Field and decided it wasn't for him. Later Mum had Liza, a huge beautiful bay. I always assumed the folk song "There's a Hole in My Bucket, Dear Liza" had been written especially for her.

For a while my parents owned a share in a racehorse called Valdez. Soon after making this investment the horse was entered into a race but Dad was advised not to waste a bet on it as the animal was inexperienced and had no chance of even being placed. Of course the animal won comfortably. After this it never won anything again, though bets were liberally placed.

My sister Emma was seriously into riding from a very young age. At age six she got her first pony called Willy, a bay Shet-

CHAPTER 12

land. At this very young age she went to her first hunt and was 'blooded'. We have a picture of her at the meet at the hunt Kennels at Eridge where my parents moved thirty years later.

Willy was followed by Ashby Darcy, a thoroughbred grey who bucked whenever anyone made a loud noise. Next came Rosie, a palomino stallion, whose full name was Pink Champagne the Third. Rosie was sold to her by Nigel Budd, a man who favoured a bowler hat when he went drag hunting and was badly injured in a fall that left him with permanent brain damage.

Emma on Willy and Celia on Liza at the Eridge Hunt meet at Bohemia where the hunt kennels were situated.

Mum and Emma trained Rosie to pull a two wheeled Gypsy trap and although they never had any bad accidents doing this, horses generally seemed to be fraught with a huge amount of danger. In just one nightmarish incident Emma was riding Rosie along by the Dovecote Inn when a stallion escaped from a property opposite and began to try and mount Rosie while Emma was still riding. She went in to the property to complain and was met by men wielding guns.

On another occasion Emma went for a ride with our neighbours, The Porters, and her horse spooked and rode clean through a five barred gate, leaving a 'pony shaped hole' in it.

GOODBYE BADSELL

The pony was later seen tearing along, apparently dragging Emma behind, although this turned out to be her picnic.

Emma and Willy, Badsell stables

Her worst accident happened while drag racing. This sport, which involved riders and hounds chasing a man rather than a fox, was even more dangerous than normal hunting because the man would deliberately choose to cross gates that were hard to jump — even ones with barbed wire on top. On one such hunt Emma got to the last jump which was a fence with a ten foot drop on the other side. Emma was the only child in the hunt and Nigel Bud and others were all cheering her and encouraging her to attempt this vast obstacle. Emma and Rosie cleared it but the jolt when the horse hit the ground was so powerful that Emma 'pecked' on landing and one of the horse's rear hooves caught her in the face, knocking a tooth out. Mum scrabbled around in the mud, found the tooth and rammed it back in.

Emma entered gymkhanas and did eventing — an incredibly

CHAPTER 12

demanding and difficult activity involving dressage, showjumping and riding cross-country courses with huge solid jumps. I often used to go and watch her at these shows and was amazed at her skill and courage. As she got more into showjumping she got a second pony called Jacob, an American saddle horse who was 'beautiful but mad'. As a show jumper Emma reached the heights of coming 'eighth in England juniors at Hickstead'. She was so tiny that she used to get a round of applause when she entered the ring.

Emma on Ashby Darcie at the Cobblers Yard Show,
Langton Green (collection of Jose Dadswell)

To enter the stables at Badsell was to enter another world. The immense cobbles had the feel of something that had been around for centuries and there were powerful evocative smells of the horses themselves, the horse food, the leather tack and the tack soap.

I was not a proper rider but riding was such a big part of farm life that inevitably I got sucked into it. I learned to clean all the tack and often accompanied Mum and Emma to riding competitions, not to mention the tack shop in Tunbridge Wells, another place with a very distinctive wonderful odour of new leather (the shop, which was by the Royal Oak on the Bayhall Road in Tunbridge Wells, vanished years ago).

For me horses were always a source of fascination and fear. It seemed to me that they were suspicious of me. This was confirmed when one of them bit me on the chest, through a jumper, and it was one of the most painful things I had ever experienced.

They always seemed to be looking at me with a startled expression. Despite this I wanted to ride and I rode a lot. I did lessons at Mrs Latini's in Five Oak Green and I did riding lessons at school. Riding lessons meant going around and around endlessly in a coral and I never seemed to improve.

I could get on a horse, I could rise to the trot, but I was always being told I was holding the reins wrong and whenever I set off on a 'hack' it generally ended badly. At some point the horse would go insane.

I remember it often happened if we broke into a canter. This lurching gait requires you to half stand in the stirrups so you don't impact the horses back. The problem was that the fact we were now going fast always seemed to drive the horse into an instant state of over-excitement and it would then break into a gallop without any instruction or encouragement from me. It might be that I was doing something wrong. Others have told me that I probably just have an 'electric bum' — a term used in riding circles to mean a rider who always gets bolted.

Up on the horse I would know the animal was bolting when the lolloping gait of the canter was replaced by the smooth coasting of a full-blown gallop combined with a dramatic increase in speed. To gallop on a horse must be absolutely exhilarating if you are in control - I imagine. For me it always spelled big trouble. The horse had changed up a gear entirely of its own accord. I would try and get the animal to stop but I would be ignored.

CHAPTER 12

I was now on a galloping horse that would not stop or even change course at my bidding. I would make increasingly desperate attempts to pull the reins but to no avail. I remember one time pulling so hard on the reins that the animals head was turned almost entirely to the side — its crazed eye looking at me — but the horse still charged along, as though even it could not control its legs.

Emma on Rosie, 30th April 1978 (Photo: John Taylor)

I vividly recall this happening at the top of the sloping field and the horse heading for the large apple tress in the old orchard. To avoid being ripped off the horse's back by the branches I had to lie flat on along the horses back, clutching its mane for dear life. By this point my feet were no longer in the stirrups, always the signal that the drama was about to reach its climax. I fell off horses at high speed many times but never broke a bone or even suffered anything more serious than a bad winding and a few bruises and scrapes.

If the animal failed to throw me then another high point of terror was crossing the little bridge at the bottom of the old orchard, followed by the humiliation of being seen by others tearing across the lawn at the front of the house and then again having to lie flat as the horse ran into the stables. Luckily most horses seemed to just want to go home.

On one occasion I was entered into a beginners class at a big horse show at Hickstead. I had dreams of glory — a rosette even — and was assured that I would barely need to do anything. Just walk around the ring, then trot, and come back to a standstill.

All went well until we trotted. In my memory somebody threw a banana skin at the horse — or near the horse. This seems highly unlikely. Maybe the reality is that somebody made a sudden move. I always had a vague feeling that what followed was not entirely my fault.

The animal spooked and broke at first into a canter then a gallop, within the relatively small space of the ring. With all the other entrants and spectators watching I tore around the ring, the horse desperately seeking an exit. Inevitably I lost my stirrups and fell, bouncing on the ground, being momentarily dragged along, then finally coming to a halt, winded and covered in mud, all in a highly formal scenario where you are meant to be displaying your control of a horse while turned out in your best riding kit.

Afterwards we all stood in a row and one by one the entrants were called forward to collect a rosette. It was a very kind and gentle event and everyone got one.

Except me. It turns out that bolting, falling, being dragged, — these things were not point winners, even in a 'beginners' event.

On the way back from Hickstead it was decided, in Ashdown Forest, that we should get the horses out and take them out for a hack. I had fallen and, as everyone knows, if you fall off a horse you are meant to get back on it.

We saddled up and headed off and I remember I was beginning to regain a smidgen of confidence when the horse's foot dropped into a hole. Now I would have thought that a horse would have taken something like that in its stride but not at all, it spooked the animal and again I found myself being bolted, this time in open, unfamiliar countryside. Again I tried to stop it but no amount of pulling the reins had any impact and again I fell. I think that might have been when I gave up riding altogether. I remember thinking, "If horses can't cope with stepping into a small hollow without going insane I don't want any more to do with them."

Celia and Emma riding at Badsell

CHAPTER 13
THE PETTING ZOO

Jose (pronounced Josie) Dadswell was born on 14 April 1961 and lived in Paddock Wood with her father and sister, her mother having died when she was just 10. They lived on a housing estate behind St. Andrew's Church.

As a child all she wanted to do was escape into the countryside and have freedom and play with horses. She and her sister, who was five years older, bullied her father to buy them a horse and they finally got their wish when Jose was about 13. The horse was called Chip.

Initially they kept Chip on some land in Matfield but when they lost access to this grazing they had to find somewhere new. Jose knew a woman called Jane Lawrence through the local riding stables. Jane knew my mother and when she heard about Jose's predicament she said she could bring her pony to the farm. This was around 1974.

After school Jose would leap on her bike and cycle from Paddock Wood to Badsell and then she would ride hop on Chip and go exploring, sometimes with my mother and later with my sister Emma and her pony Darcy. In the endless summer heatwave of 1976 they would tie the horses up at the Porter's house

CHAPTER 13

on Colt's Hill. While the horses cooled off in the shade they would have a swim.

Jose with Chip and Darcie in the Horse Field in the 1970s (Photo: collection of Jose Twynam)

Jose credits these experiences with building confidence and independence but Chip wasn't always the easiest of ponies.

He was mostly fine just riding around the farm. He didn't buck but occasionally he'd take hold of the bit and take off - he was a bolter. On roads he was particularly dangerous. If he saw a lorry or a tractor coming he would try and turn the other way. Jose was always being thrown off and so were her friends. When Rosie was bought for my sister, a replacement for Darcie, Chip took a dislike to her and chased her all over the horse field. Finally Rosie leaped over a five barred gate to get away from her tormentor after which Rosie was seen hobbling away, holding a leg in the air. It was a rare moment when Mum lost her cool and Jose was reduced to tears.

Things were soon looking up though when Jose's father built a bungalow at nearby Five Oak Green. They had five acres of land and finally Jose had somewhere to keep Chip. By this time Badsell was like a second home to Jose and she was almost part of our family, coming to many of our social gatherings including the Christening of John and Charles.

Through Badsell, Jose had been developing an interest in farming and seeing my mother running Badsell inspired her. In those days a woman farmer was a rare thing but Jose could see that Mum had a good life, an active social life and was able to keep her own horses. Jose thought, "I'd like a slice of that!"

In fact she wasn't the only person Mum encouraged to go to agricultural college. She encouraged Brian Wiseman to go to Hadlow College to study agriculture but his father, Ernie, warned him off by saying, "There's no money in farming."

To get into agricultural college Jose had to work for a year at a dairy farm at Castle Hill. Then she went off to Seale Hayne agricultural college in Devon.

During this period Jose's father passed away and her stepmother sold the bungalow in Five Oak Green. By this time she had a horse called Corey and while working at another dairy farm, this time in Somerset, Corey had a foal. When that job came to an end Jose was of 'no fixed abode' and, once again, in need of somewhere to keep her much-adored horses. As she puts it, "Who should come to my rescue but your mum!"

By this time Jose had a regular boyfriend called Chris who is now her husband. Together they visited Cotswold Farm Park, run by Adam Henson, who today is a familiar face on the BBC programme Country File.

Jose thought the concept of a rare breed farm park could work for Badsell so she raised the idea with my parents. She suggested that, with the public already coming onto the farm to pick fruit, having some animals as an attraction could be a way to earn more income. My mum was immediately enthusiastic, saying it was an idea she had already thought about, but Dad was a little more circumspect. He asked Jose to prove her commitment by working at Badsell through the summer, and he also asked her to come up with a few figures — in other words a 'business plan.'

Jose did a sort of cash flow and management plan, putting to use some of the things that she had learned at college. She showed she had a vision for the place and she got the go-ahead to start and she and Mum began collecting animals, starting with a few rabbits and chickens.

When the 'rare breeds park' first opened the charge was one Pound a person and it was not easy to persuade anyone to go in. Jose would have to practically drag people in, saying, "Come and see our animals, I'll take you around."

Early poster advertising Badsell's petting zoo

By 1984 a Gloucester Old Spot pig called Penelope had been added, as had 10 Soay sheep from Penshurst Vineyard. Soon they were joined by two Wensleydale sheep, a middle white pig called Gutsy, purchased from Ashurst, and four goats, whose names all began with an 'I' (Ida, Isla , Irma and Iris, who was almost blind). These were purchased from what was known as the 'Mad Goat Lady of Itham'. We always had a lot of goats and there was a Guernsey goat whose kids had a habit of climbing into pushchairs. We also had pygmy goats called Lilly and Holly and an Anglo Nubian goat called Beth, (with a very loud voice).

Jose with Gutsy, the middle white pig and her piglets in the coral in the petting zoo

Bambi, a Guernsey calf, grew up on the farm and later had a calf called Velvet. On one occasion a little boy who had come to the farm as part of a school trip, was learning about milking when he put up his hand and asked, "Where do the burgers come out?"

Later a highland bull called Yogi arrived and young Nick Belton used to enjoy riding him 'like a motorbike'. He also used to ride a particularly aggressive ram because, as he pointed out, it was safer to ride it than be attacked by it. I often used to ride Penelope, the huge Gloucester Old Spot pig, although it was hazardous. I would sit on her rump and she would immediately charge - galloping at full speed until I came off. Another favourite pastime with Penelope was lobbing sweet apples high into the air from a distance so that they landed near her. She had no idea where these apples were coming from, why they appeared to be falling out of a clear blue sky, but she gobbled them up regardless. Penelope is now immortalised on the wind vane of the cowl of the oast house at Badsell, cut out in steel by Andy Browning from a drawing by myself.

Bambi in the bullock barn with Velvet, her calf,
(photo: Jose Twynam)

We had a handsome little chestnut Shetland stallion called Peanut. Georgie Belton used to ride him and he was 'gorgeous' but he occasionally liked to escape in order to visit the Gypsy ponies at the Traveller site at Cinder Hill. Nick Belton remembers riding him and, because the saddle hadn't been done up tightly, he slipped around so that he was hanging upside down, just as they went over a jump. Another pony we owned was Bertie, who was purchased by Mum at the Horsmonden Traveller fair.

We had various donkeys including Jasper who was white and Barncy, who once escaped with his friend and headed up to Matfield on Crittenden Lane.

People often brought animals to Badsell and at one point three baby squirrels arrived. Their drey had fallen out of a tree and they were still pink. The Belton's hand fed them and had to wear the kind of gauntlet used by falconers to stop being scratched and bitten. Later they lived in a large hexagonal cage at Badsell and were eventually released.

One day someone rang Gail and said they had a "French

Street Owl". She imagined this owl turning up in a beret but it turned out to be a screech owl. For a while Alan Ames used to keep birds of prey at the farm and did displays of falconry.

Gail Belton (left) with Sarah Walter with Jasper pulling the cart at the Badsell Park Fayre

We had ducks, golden pheasants, quail and guinea fowl. We had pigmy goats, a Billy goat, inevitably called 'Billy', Beth and Duncan (a pair of Vietnamese pot Bellied pigs) and later a large pot bellied pig called Mycroft.

Mum was very fond of chickens and naturally enough, a rare breeds farm was the perfect place to indulge a fondness for poultry. She became a subscriber to 'Fancy Fowl' magazine, and we all became adept at naming all the different breeds. My favourites were the Polish bantams with their extraordinary shock of white feathers jutting out from the tops of their heads.

CHAPTER 13

For some reason, in the early days, ours often had bald patches on top (probably from being pecked by other chickens) which made them look like monks in need of a trim. Of course we also loved the silkies with their feathers that look like fluffy fur (they remind me of tiny two legged llamas) and the beautiful black and white Appenzeller Spitzhauben. There were also the Buff Orpingtons and Speckled Sussex which were much larger.

A publicity shot featuring (from right) Jose Dadswell, Liz Tizzard, Liz's daughter, and Celia Preston

The various breeds were displayed in separate enclosures in the chicken barn - at first - but over the years it has to be said that inbreeding went on and gradually everything became a bit diluted. And of course we always had several basic 'layers' - just big chickens, of various colours, who were let out every day and hung about pecking at the ground and taking advantage of any eating opportunities that arose. This group of chickens became known as The Street Gang.

A guest at one of our many parties was a character called Phil Dirtbox, a friend of my sister Emma's, and, as was traditional, he hung about the following day with the compulsory hangover. Phil had a very distinctive look - bowler hat, DM boots and suit trousers with braces. He was extremely tall and imposing but he was a poet at heart and The Street Gang inspired him.

He loved the concept of a mob of unruly mongrel chickens and he composed probably his best poem which, at the time of writing, has been lost, but which I hope will one day take its place in the cannon of world literature. I can only remember snatches such as 'They are the Street Gang, the white meat gang" "They are well out of order, last seen on the Kent/Sussex border" and "never laid an egg in their lives..."

Badsell became a place where we could pursue any passion or interest as long as it lead to some sort of attraction being added to the place. Mum loved anyone who pursued one of the old country crafts - people who worked with wood, people who built in traditional ways. While at Badsell she rescued a beautifully crafted ancient wooden waggon, of the type that was once ubiquitous in the countryside but which are almost all gone. When we left the farm she insisted on bringing it to her next home and, conscious that the elements were starting to affect it, she sought out people who valued and preserved these wagons and made sure it got safely into a museum.

Dad had been interested in moths and caterpillars since he was a boy and he now had the perfect excuse to start breeding again. Initially he had containers on display in the pet shed with magnificent caterpillars chomping away on leaves. We usually had a few stick insects as well, which always ate privet. Conveniently we had a large privet hedge between the back and front gardens of the farmhouse. For a while we had a magnificent giant stick insect but sadly it died. It was quickly realised that it was exactly as entertaining dead as it had been alive and it remained on display, drawing admiration for several years.

CHAPTER 13

The ancient farm waggon on display at Badsell.

Later Dad created a butterfly house. My favourite was always the Elephant Hawk moth. When the caterpillars are fully grown they are magnificent, great fat grey/brown things with huge fake eyes. After their metamorphosis they become stunning pink and green moths which, in the wild, are entirely nocturnal and therefore almost never seen. We all grew familiar with this hidden world because my father had (and still has) a thing like a crude flying saucer from a low budget 1950s sci-fi film. This moth trap was often set on summer evenings and in the morning we would wonder at the variety of moths that had been lured in to hide amongst the egg boxes. Dad knows all the names. My favourite is the Setatious Hebrew Character. On one occasion the local TV news came to cover his opening of the moth trap but unfortunately a swarm of wasps were attacking the contents. The reporter just cowered in terror at a distance.

Initially there wasn't really enough income from the 'rare breeds park' to pay Jose through the year so she would go off and do other farming work like lambing. She had many friends in the farming world and in particular in the sheep world and one of the first events that was held at the farm was a Spinning Day. Various women set up their spinning wheels in the pet area and, to add to the attractions, a sheep shearing demonstration was also advertised.

A young man that Jose had been lambing for was going to come to the farm and sheer all the sheep but when the day arrived he did not turn up because he was having marital problems and a nervous breakdown. Jose remembers my father becoming quite upset at this 'no show' and she announced that she wouldn't let him down. She drove off to Benenden where the man lived and ordered him to pull himself together, go to Badsell and sheer sheep, which he did.

Joyce Miles at the 'Wool Day,' one of the first events held at the farm (Photo: Jose Twynam)

On one occasion Jose had to drive Penelope, the Gloucester Old Spot, to Dormansland so that she could be bred with a boar. Driving along the A264 from East Grinstead to Tunbridge Wells she heard a commotion coming from the horse box. The Badsell horse box had a 'jockey door' and she could see that it was moving.

By the time Jose stopped the vehicle, the pig was standing in the middle of the A264 at five o'clock on a weekday. An elderly couple stopped to help but didn't get out of their car. Instead they used their vehicle as a cowboy might use a horse to drive the pig back to the trailer. Once Jose got the pig inside she had to stand with her back to the jockey door holding it closed while

CHAPTER 13

the couple then drove to the nearest phone. They called the man at the farm where she had just been to collect the pig and he came out with some wood and a hammer and nails and he barricaded up the door. When Jose got back to the farm Mum poured her a big gin and tonic.

Being Badsell the Jockey door was never properly repaired and a few months later the same thing happened again, but this time it was Mum who was driving the pig, and she actually got a conviction from the Police for breaking some archaic law about having an animal on a road.

Animal escapes were fairly common. There was a Soay sheep called Barbara who was very canny. Soay are a very wild breed anyway but with Barbara leading them they were impossible to control. For a while we kept them through the winter at our friends the Frank's place in Matfield. Barbara lead them on an escape and they were finally tracked down to the Charrington's farm a couple of miles away. One of them was never found and is presumed to have entered the 'wild stock'.

Having so many animals meant there was a lot of life and death. One of the strawberry pickers who lived in Paddock Wood asked Jose if she could re-home her pet rabbit at Badsell because her children had lost interest in it. One day the woman visited the pet area and asked to see how the rabbit was getting on. Jose lead her and her children to the pen, only to find the animal lying prostrate with advanced rigour mortis. As Jose puts it, "It was very awkward."

Although initially Jose was keen to make Badsell a rare breeds park we gradually moved away from that as the pressure was on to just have a lot of different and ideally friendly animals.

Jose had a dog called Poppy who had free range of the place. One time Joan Piper, a lady who worked on the farm for several years, made several strawberry flans for a Strawberry Festival.

She had piped whipped cream all over them but Jose noticed that they were all only half covered in cream. She suddenly realised that Poppy had licked the cream off the ones she could reach and it became even more obvious when the dog threw up all the cream in front of Dad. Jose had to break the news to Joan who took the flans home, repiped them with cream and brought them back again.

The pet area had several loyal season ticket holders and Jose still meets people, now in their 40's, who went to Badsell as children and loved the place. Many still have photos of the animals or pictures of themselves and their friends at birthday parties.

Badsell was occasionally used as a location for filming and featured on a show called Codzmorf which was about a father who turned inanimate objects into animals. The location was chosen for obvious reasons - we had lots of animals, but animals had to be brought in for the production as well, including an elephant.

Many of the staff on the farm got involved in this production and Gail Belton remembers waiting for ages in my bedroom with two goat kids while the crew set up the next shot. What was very popular was the food truck which kept everyone plied with bacon sarnies.

An elephant visiting Badsell for the filming of 'Codzmorf'

CHAPTER 13

One of the things we came up with to 'add value' to the experience of visiting the farm was an animal parade on the front lawn in front of the house. By this point the lawn had been fenced which allowed us to use it as additional pasture for sheep and ponies.

Of course a person leading a goat around a patch of grass is not particularly interesting so I was charged with coming up with an amusing commentary. The idea was to introduce the animal's name, talk about the breed, the peculiarities of the individual and any other thoughts or ideas (or jokes) that could make it entertaining. I felt the responsibility of this keenly and on a Sunday morning I sat at the dining table in the farmhouse, with a blank piece of paper, trying to think of something to say about each animal. We had a house guest and I can remember them asking my mother what I was doing. "He's writing a commentary for the animal parade" I heard her say. Then she dropped her voice to a whisper, "He takes these things very seriously."

A film crew at work on the front lawn

In her mind writing it down showed an eccentric level of keenness but there was another problem I faced which made having a cheat sheet even more essential. We had a fairly primitive public address system which was mainly used to call members of staff (I would occasionally come on and say "Would Rupert Preston please get that bucket".)

If you wanted to provide commentary for an animal parade it was not ideal because the microphone was situated inside the gift shop in the main oast with no extension lead and no view of the front lawn. I had to set up a system of hand signals with someone standing at the entrance - even though, because of a line of poplar trees, they also had no view and had to run back and forth to the lawn. The result was that my witty commentary was often about the wrong animal. The only one I can recall was the blind millefleur chicken, known as Peckie, which was carried in by someone, probably Gail, and I tugged the heart strings of the audience by talking about her trusting ways.

When Jose took maternity leave Gail Belton filled in as manager of the pet area, but as she recalls it, "I just kind of ended up working there."

Gail had grown up at Palace Farm at Doddington in East Kent and aged ten had moved to another farm, Owletts, near Lamberhurst. She had grown up with farm animals and used to visit Badsell with her children, Georgie and Nick, when they were small.

Gail Belton in the Kent and Sussex Courier

CHAPTER 13

By the time they were five and seven she had started working there. One day Jose said to her, as they were walking around the pet area "Do you think you could do this? Would you like to do this job?" Gail was unsure but Jose pointed out that she had a farming background and knew about animals. As Gail puts it today: "I don't actually remember what happened, but before I knew it, I was running the pet area. And Jose had gone."

Gail describes working at Badsell as, "Some of the best days of my life. It was such good fun. It was just so free and easy." One happy memory was on the 'balloon day' when a large number of balloons took off from the Park Field. Gail got to ride in one and the fact that it hit the clock tower at Mascalls School in Paddock Wood, and she nearly died, didn't make it any less thrilling. When she started working in the pet area there was a new arrival - Lopez the llama - and she went to see him in his stable near the pig sty. He immediately bit her on the head.

Ready for take off. Gail and Nick Belton on the 'Balloon Day'

She particularly loved Badsell because Georgie and Nick

could come to work with her. There was no need to pay childcare costs because the kids were simply allowed to run wild on the farm, and Gail was not the only mother to benefit from this. Angie Mead, who ended up keeping many horses on the farm, would just put her baby son Rupert down in the strawberry patch behind the stables. She would leave him there, crawling about eating strawberries while she did the mucking out, then she or one of her daughters, Nico or Carlie, would go and collect him. He would of course be covered in strawberry juice.

Later Gail's daughter Georgie got to keep her pony Polly at Badsell and she spent her days riding. One day she was out hacking with her friend Sarah Long who was on a pony called Coffee. Coffee threw Sarah and Georgie rode Polly all the way back to the farm and *into* the café where she reported the accident.

Any ponies on the farm had to earn their keep by doing pony rides which took place on the big lawn in front of the farmhouse. These rides were extremely popular with visitors but it was a pain to do. Endlessly leading ponies around in circles is boring and the ponies didn't particularly like it either. Everyone was constantly being ordered to 'go and do some pony rides' and trying to get out of it.

Gail's daughter Georgie describes the Badsell days as "the best of days" and adds, "I had such a great time growing up at Badsell". She learned to be a shepherd, to do the lambing and to milk the goats. Her brother Nick was allowed to do whatever he wanted. He remembers, on one occasion, tying up Sean Wiseman, Brian's son, because he was being a pain. "It was just over the bridge from the blackberries, at the bottom of the sloping field, we tied him to a tree and left him there'.

Nick was also introduced, by the 'terrible twins' to the terrifying climb up to the 'secret den' at the top of the oast.

CHAPTER 13

Georgie Belton on Polly. The Badsell van is in the background

Later he kept motorbikes at the farm and got to muck about in non-street legal cars which appeared to just 'belong to everybody'. He learned to drive a tractor by the age of ten and was being sent off to pick up bales of straw to bring them to the pet area. The Belton children could even bring their friends to Gail's work and, as Gail puts it, "Their friends were queuing up - asking - 'can we come to work with your mum?'"

These days the influence of Badsell on both Gail's children is obvious - Nick works at a large farm near Horsmonden and Georgie has a menagerie of rescued poultry in her garden.

Gail's husband, Bob, also worked at Badsell where he was able to apply experience that he'd had with horses in Zermatt in Switzerland. In his teens and early twenties he had worked giving sleigh rides. For a while at Badsell he gave carriage rides to visitors. Bob was also the maintenance man on the farm for three or four years. His son Nick remembers him, on a rainy day, with a big pot of bent nails, straightening them out with a hammer.

Gail particularly appreciated my Dad's sense of humour

and remembers him tucking into what he thought was a rather low grade paté in the farmhouse kitchen, then realising it was dog food, and announcing that it was "fairly decent". He also appeared one day holding what appeared to be a dead chamois Polish hen under one arm. Gail witnessed as he announced to Mum that it was dead, much to her shock and horror. He then pulled it out to reveal that it was a feather duster. She also members Dad entering the pen of 'Benny the Bastard', a huge Barnvelder cockerel which attacked him savagely, as it did everyone.

Dad's sense of humour is somewhat legendary and probably reached its apotheosis one morning when, finding that the fridge in the farmhouse was bare, he went across to his own café and ordered a full English breakfast.

He was seated outside on a sunny morning and several of us joined him. After biting into one of the large, cheap, 'ironclad' sausages that the chef ordered frozen in bulk from the Cash and Carry, my father paused reflectively and finally announced "In the darkest hours of the war, British Rail served a better sausage than that."

He has pointed out since, rather pedantically, that 'British Rail' did not exist during the war, but to list the various regional companies would have spoiled the timing.

One of Dad's favourite sayings was 'if a job is worth doing, it is worth doing badly.' For him this was a passport to fix everything with nails and bailer twine. It was a slightly aristocratic disdain for taking things too seriously and applying yourself to tasks with unseemly keenness.

The fact that the cages and fences and doors and signposts were all often built or mended with a few odd nails and some bailer twine meant that there were a lot of minor incidents. If a danger presented itself we would find a quick fix that would avert danger for that week — or that day. When it was noted

CHAPTER 13

that customers were hand feeding the pigs, which are capable of taking off a finger, no effort was made to improve the fencing, I was just told to write some warning notices. I used a black marker pen to draw a picture of someone with stubs where their hands should be, with severed dismembered hands lying about on the grass. It seemed to do the trick.

Having a petting zoo meant that Dad could indulge his interest in insects. One day a man appeared at the front door of the farmhouse with a small white plastic bottle. It was, he claimed, everything you needed to create a tropical Trinidadian leaf-cutter ant colony. Dad simply could not resist buying this thing which came with a detailed booklet of instructions.

The booklet was brought into the kitchen and he began to read it out loud. "First" it read. "you will need to build a fully insulated tropical ant house with double glazed viewing windows." It went on to describe how the ants would need a large glass tank in which they would build their underground 'garden'. The tank would need to be moated to keep them in. The ants would then climb up a rope, suspended from the ceiling with cat gut (which they allegedly could not climb) on to floating wooden platforms, also suspended by cat gut, onto which we would pile their food which would include leaves, petals and even ham. The ants would carry their food back to their tank and grow nutritious mould in their underground garden.

Now of course all this was very expensive but having bought the colony we were committed, so sure enough two thousand pounds later, we had a tropical ant house.

It was indeed a fascinating thing. The ants reproduced exponentially and after a while you could indeed glimpse ants crawling along the ropes through the viewing windows. It was much more interesting, however, to go inside, which unfortunately the public could not do.

We in the family, and the various workers on the farm, could enter the tropical ant house. The sight of the ants swarming up the ropes was fascinating in close up and there was the added benefit that, in the midst of winter, it was the only properly heated interior on the entire farm.

At least one person tried to sleep in there at one of our many parties but this was not possible because soon 'the odd stray ant' became a swarm. The ants were not satisfied with the limitations placed on them by the moat and the cat gut and they became obsessed with escape. They began flinging themselves bodily into the moat by the thousands, creating a bridge of their own corpses. Once this was built they swarmed across to 'freedom'. They soon found their way out of the building itself and established a new home outside in the English countryside. This feral colony thrived for one summer then was nuked by the English winter.

CHAPTER 14
THE MOUSE HOUSE

One day I was gripped by the idea of creating my own attraction at the farm. My idea was that I would build a big dolls house and have mice living in it. I started building it in the old shed where, many years before, a man had told me that my hands might spontaneously burst into flames. My vision for this attraction was quite grand.

I saw it as a mouse mansion and I wanted it to be a delight for the viewer. The chief pleasure would be in seeing the mice living in great splendour and comfort and it would be impossible not to think of them as a bunch of wild party animals — because they would appear to be perpetually feasting at a great table. Wherever they were in the house there would be the sense that they were characters in an ongoing drama about a wild night in a grand house.

At that time there was a shop in Hastings that sold dolls house furnishings and fittings. They had everything from little table lamps to glowing fires to sofas and chairs, baths, toilets — the full works — all to scale and, as I recall, not too expensive as it was all made in China. So although I made a lot of the fixtures and fittings, such as the grand sweeping staircase, I also had a lot of very impressive things from this shop, such as working lamps, victorian baths and sofas and chairs.

In the basement I created a sort of dark arched area which was only very dimly lit. this was out of consideration for the mice. I felt it was unfair to expose them to too much electric light all day — they had to have somewhere that was a bit gloomy and 'private'.

Next floor up was an old fashioned kitchen complete with a glowing fire. I made a joint of meat out of paper maché (I used strips of paper cut up from a large photograph of Robert DeNiro's face which was the right colour.) This leg of meat rotated over the fire, driven by a mouse wheel.

Next up was the grand dining room. I made a long dining table and had little chairs all the way down the length of it and at both ends. Little plates were glued to the table which was stained a dark brown and varnished, and little wine bottles and glasses were also glued along the length of the table. The mice were fed on the plates on the table.

On the walls I created framed mouse portraits, which I painted myself with a tiny brush. On the top floor was a bedroom with a four poster bed and a bathroom with a bath which was used to give the mice water.

Throughout the house were working light fittings ranging from a grand chandelier to little table lamps. Once the mouse house was installed in the roundel, which was completely dark when the door was shut, the public were able to enjoy something quite magical. The whole thing had a glass front and the back opened on hinges so that we could sweep up the droppings and replenish food and water relatively easily.

I was ably assisted in building the mouse house by Wendela Von Munching - or Wendy as she was known to us. She first came to Badsell as the girlfriend of Andy, one of Lizzie Rogers sons. As was often the way with Badsell she fell in love the place

CHAPTER 14

and eventually saw Mum as a sort of additional mother figure in her life, as several people did.

The mice themselves came from different sources. Samantha, my brothers wife, remembers me asking her to buy mice in a shop in Camden Town in London. She purchased ten of them and drove them back to her flat in Notting Hill, but they chewed through the cardboard box and she had to cope with ten mice running loose in her car while she drove. Other mice came from Nick and Georgie Belton who had started breeding them at home. They used to sell them to their friends at school but the friends would quickly be told by their parents that they could not keep mice. So Nick and Georgie would offer to look after them for them — charging rent for the service. A great little racket!

Once the mice were installed the mouse house came alive but not everyone was happy. The chef in the cafe announced that he did not like mice and having a mouse house in the building made him nervous. Someone then rubbed him up the wrong way by putting a rubber mouse in his *Bain Marie*.

To this day — about thirty-five years later - I still meet people who remember the mouse house as something special. People did not have camera phones in those days and not a single image has survived. Even if you had a camera it was hard to photograph because, if you took a picture with a flash, the light just bounced off the glass, and without a flash it was way too dark.

Sadly the local 'Health and Safety' tyrant from Tunbridge Wells Borough Council put paid to the mouse house. When they were doing one of their inspections they noted that the Mouse House was in the same building as the café (though they were separated by a very large gift shop). We were ordered to remove the mouse house and it was taken to a shed known as the 'Information Room' which had a transparent corrugated plastic roof. This was the room you had to pass through to enter the petting zoo and it was where people bought paper bags full of feed which would immediately be devoured by the first goat they encountered in the pet area.

Being lit up by daylight the mouse house lost its visual impact. Another problem was that the mice chewed everything — so all the little sofas, chairs and tables very rapidly began to shrink. The glory days of the Mouse House lasted only a few short months in a single summer when it was in all its glory the oast house — but those who saw it never forgot it!

CHAPTER 15
SNAIL RACING SCANDAL!

At its height Badsell Park Farm was attracting about 50,000 visitors a year but the need to promote the place was unrelenting and Mum and Dad were constantly worried that not enough visitors were coming and there was not enough for them to see.

We placed a regular ad in the Kent and Sussex Courier but the promotions budget was pretty minimal. At one point we made a video about the many attractions on the farm. It was expertly directed by John Rogers (who would go on to work at Miramax, reediting films for Harvey Weinstein). It was great fun to make and my Godfather, Patrick Mercheson provided a lively voice over but we never thought about where the video was going to be shown and it languished amongst our collection of VHS cassettes.

The solution that we came up with was to get the farm into the press by creating stories.

Somehow a character called Allan Breeze found his way into our lives and he became the maestro of Badsell bullshit. He would literally make something up and pitch it to my Dad. He would then tell the press and, if they nibbled, we would be ordered to make it happen. In 1993 he came up with the idea that our pigs watched the Queen's speech on Christmas Day.

An early advertisement for Badsell in the Kent and Sussex Courier

The local TV news, Newsroom South East, lapped up this upbeat Christmas story which was destined for the end of their news programme. In order to give them a visual story, we had to set up a VHS player and TV in the pig sty, so that we could play the previous year's Queen's speech for the pigs.

The TV crew turned up and filmed the story but the only person available to appear on camera was Mum, who was incredibly busy. When the piece appeared on the early evening news she did her level best to persuade viewers that the pigs loved watching the Queen's speech on Christmas Day, but she looked like she had more important things on her mind.

The following year Allan had another brainwave and announced that we had the luckiest turkey in the world. Named 'Lucky' this turkey not only was not going to be eaten on Christmas Day - it was invited to Christmas lunch. Good Morning Britain took the bait and again the whole scene had to be faked in advance of Christmas Day. Martin Frizzel was the presenter and again none of us were around to be filmed for a fake Christmas lunch. Angie Mead, who did horse and cart

CHAPTER 15

rides, played the 'mother' and Georgie and Nick Belton played the children and they all sat around our dining table. Gail then brought the huge live turkey in. In fact so popular was this story that the scene had to be staged more than once.

From The Sun newspaper, 1993

Years later, while travelling in America, my brother John saw the turkey story at Badsell presented as 'news' on a local TV station in California.

Another story that Allan came up with was that Badsell was a home for retired Scarecrows. Dad created a press release, sending it out from his PR office in London. When a news organisation showed interest he ordered us all to make scarecrows. These were then nailed to posts all along the drive, so that it looked like some hideous version of the Appian Way after Spartacus' failed slave revolt of 71 BC.

Of all the stories that Allan came up with by far the most successful was his snail racing 'scandal'.

This involved the pretence that we were running regular snail races at the farm. The story was that snails were being doped with beer to 'hobble' them and the referee had developed a technique for testing the snails by licking them.

'Luckiest turkey' story in the Daily Star

This story excited interest globally and Dad found himself doing radio interviews with stations as far away as Australia and South Africa - interviews which were, in publicity terms, a waste of time as nobody was going to travel from those parts to a petting zoo in England. Dad also found himself on a German game show in which contestants had to guess your profession. If they failed there was a large cash prize on offer. Of course Dad went out to Germany confident that nobody was going to guess he was a snail race referee because:

1. There is no such thing as a snail race referee.
2. He wasn't one.

Despite this a German contestant guessed the right answer

almost immediately, making Dad suspect that the whole thing was revenge for German's defeat in the Second World War.

In advance of the filming of the show in Germany they sent a camera crew to the farm where they filmed a snail race in the gift shop. I came and watched for a minute and was told by the German director that I was in shot and would therefore need to commit to standing there for hours. I quietly slipped away, leaving several members of staff pretending to be genuine spectators, including William Mcinally, Andy Browning and Mark Lucas. For some reason Mike Cushing, the son of the famous actor Peter Cushing, was also there with his wife.

Simon starting a snail race in the farm shop

So big was the snail racing story that Dad was invited on to ITV's breakfast programme and shortly afterwards he sought me out and asked me if I would do The Big Breakfast on Channel 4 as they wanted to do the same story on the same morning. I had worked a bit in the television industry and I knew that there might be an issue with two channels covering the same story but my objections were overruled.

I was living at the time in Clapton in East London and a car was sent for me by The Big Breakfast at dawn. I had a can of Tennents Extra beer, several giant African land snails and a snail racing canvas with a big round target painted on it.

I was extremely anxious. Not only was the whole story a complete fabrication but I had never officiated at a snail race and the (invented) technique for testing if the snails were doped with beer was to lick them. I would not want to lick any snail but a giant African land snail is a massive thing with a huge slimy body. The thought of licking it was making me ill. The thought of licking it live on national TV then identifying the wrong snail, because I had never licked a snail before (and would be too busy gagging to actually reflect on the flavour), terrified me.

I found myself seated in the green room at the Big Breakfast studio which was in the old lock-keepers cottages on Fish Island in Bow. There was a TV set fixed high up in the corner of the room showing the rival ITV breakfast show and after a while it started showing images of Dad, chatting away and bearing the exact same equipment as me — the snails, the beer, the target. An ashen-faced producer walked in and asked "Is that your father on ITV doing the same story?"

"Is that a problem?" I asked and was ordered to leave immediately. No taxi was offered but I have never felt relief like it.

Not long after this my father appeared on the local news again. This time the story was about how he had been seconded into SIS, the precursor of MI6, the secret services, and had served undercover in Austria in the 1950s, preparing the ground for the expected Soviet invasion of Western Europe.

To enliven the story the local news producer decided to film

CHAPTER 15

the piece as though Dad was the real James Bond, complete with the bond theme and some nonsense about how he took his Martini shaken not stirred.

Simon at the Imperial War Museum in front of the exhibit about his secret work for MI6 in Austria in the 1950s

In fact this story was completely true and the Imperial War Museum was launching a new exhibition called The Secret War. MI6 had agreed to release details about Dad and a friend of his called Michael Gyles who had both been seconded from the Royal Marines when they were nineteen. The Secret War featured an extensive exhibit about Dad's exploits which remained on display for over twenty years.

At that time I went to visit my dentist in Hadlow and as he examined my teeth he said, "I see your father's on the news again — pretending to be a spy this time."

GOODBYE BADSELL

A sample of press cuttings about the 'snail racing scandal' at Badsell

CHAPTER 16
EXIT THROUGH THE GIFT SHOP

The gift shop had all sorts of stuff — basically anyone with the gumption to travel to the farm and do a sales pitch to whoever happened to be in charge at that moment, would soon find their wares for sale. What sold best were small plastic animals and other toys for small children, but not everything sold well. One man turned up with a load of toys but when he returned to find that nothing had sold he was flung into an instant existential crisis, in a miniature Kentish version of 'Death off a Salesman'.

One lady called Janet made and sold candles, some of them mildly erotic, and was known, ever afterwards, as 'Janet the Candle'. Thirty years later she was still working with my parents helping them to administer the pet cemetery, and still referred to as 'Janet the Candle'.

I tried selling a few things myself - a limited edition etching of a Vietnamese pot bellied pig (I never sold one) a couple of T-shirts I designed for the 'Badsell Park Fayre' (all eventually shoplifted), and my collection of toy farm machinery (all sold). Andy and Mark, who did a lot of construction on the farm, tried selling animal hutches in the shop but they quickly realised they couldn't compete with mass produced hutches on price.

You could even buy wine in the gift shop which was unusual in the 1970's as the great British public were not yet wine drinkers on a mass scale. A friend of my fathers, John Watt, who lived in Cornwall, had a business importing wine from Brittany. The wine was very crude French plonk.

The gift shop (photo: Jose Dadswell)

Due to licensing restrictions we were only allowed to sell it by the crate but there was a small clientele who beat a path to our door to get their hands on the stuff. One man from Paddock Wood bought it regularly because it reminded him of his youth in Northern France. He swore by it but barely anyone else could drink it. My parents were enthusiastic wine drinkers and they were usually happy with the lower priced red or white from the local supermarket. Sometimes they would find they had nothing to drink and it would be announced, with regret, that someone would have to go 'over to the oast' to get a bottle of the stuff they were selling to the public.

To supply the farm with additional products Mum got into jam and jelly making. This involved boiling vast pans full of whatever fruit was involved - blackberries, strawberries, crab apples (for jelly) and adding serious amounts of sugar. For jellies

CHAPTER 16

she then hung a muslin cloth from a hook in the middle of the kitchen ceiling and it would drip away for hours. Mum also made fudge and coconut icing which was half white and half pink and was sold in transparent bags. Of course we had unlimited access to the stuff and ate mountains of it.

Because we had the shop and the cafe we had a 'Cash and Carry' card which meant we could shop at the vast 'shop for shopkeepers' in the North Farm estate outside Tunbridge Wells. This place always amazed me, chiefly because you could buy whole slabs of Coca Cola cans, whole boxes of Mars and Marathon bars and a thousand other children's dreams come true.

Celia making blackberry and apple jelly in the farmhouse kitchen

I loved going to the Cash and Carry with Mum because it was relatively easy to persuade her to add a slab of sweets to the trolley. One time I noticed a yellow racing bike hanging high up on the wall for sale at a bargain price. My birthday was coming up and the bike was purchased.

We actually sold some sweets in the farm shop and we quickly realised that, with no proper stock taking, we could slip in and pinch a chocolate bar without any consequences. This lack of normal oversight of stock meant there was a great deal of pilfering which can't have helped profits. Even quite large items like clothing would vanish at an alarming rate, but my parents had a rather innocent attitude to humanity and did not really accept that it was going on. Only when they realised one day that actual animals were disappearing from the pet area did they try and clamp down a bit.

We lost a lot through theft at Badsell and not just from the gift shop. There were many burglaries. On at least one occasion the farmhouse was robbed of the Saturday takings while we all slept. The horse tack was stolen from the stables and another time all the food was taken from the freezers in the oast house. I think that was the time the thieves opened some of the wine we sold by the crate, drank some and promptly threw up. The next day the police were there 'investigating' when my sister found a lollipop stick. Deducing that one of the thieves had eaten it during the robbery, she took it to the policeman and suggested he check it for finger prints. She was only little and he leaned down in a hideously patronising way and said "yes that's right we're going to catch the robbers aren't we little girl." She was furious.

The thing that was stolen most often was the Honda three wheeler motorbike, maybe the thieves were concerned for our safety. These vanished almost every year, despite always being locked away at night. It was clearly a favourite item for whoever was taking it - easy to sell and, having no number plate, impossible to trace.

CHAPTER 16

Simon in the farm shop when it was in the roundel. Bags of Celia's homemade fudge and coconut icing are visible, as is one of the paper bags promoting English fruit.

CHAPTER 17
CHRISTMAS IS CANCELLED

CHRISTMAS AT BADSELL WAS INEVITABLY A VERY MAGICAL time for us as a family but we provided something quite special for the public as well.

Once the pet area was established and we had a café and gift shop we started remaining open later in the year and eventually we remained open in the lead up to Christmas.

Although the roundel was initially used as the farm shop this moved across the yard to what had once been the dark and smelly engineering workshop. Meanwhile a huge sprawling gift shop was established in the barn attached to the roundel. This meant the roundel became redundant but at Christmas it hosted one of the best Santa's Grottos anywhere.

We would create a mini forest of Christmas trees and cover the ground with fake snow. We then brought in real animals - rabbits, Peckie the blind Millefleur chicken, a donkey, and Santa would sit in a tiny grove within the forest. The whole scene was lit by a few carefully directed spotlights and, because there were large gaps between the thin wood planks above (over which the hops had once been lain when it had been a drying kiln) we were able to make it snow continuously by having someone

CHAPTER 17

standing up in the 'reek' sprinkling fake snow whenever a child appeared.

However the *piéce de la resistance* were Santa's little helpers. When The Twins were about nine year's old they agreed to be elves and someone produced a pair of rubber elf masks which covered the upper part of their faces, meaning that their mouths moved, making them utterly convincing.

The role of Santa was shared amongst the grown up males and I performed the role many times. My abiding memory is that I would be seated in the grotto, with my elves standing either side of me, and a child would wander in. Obviously smaller children came in with their parents but over the age of about six or seven they would be shoved in alone. Children as old as nine would come in, already skeptical about the existence of Santa, and pretty damned certain that this spit and sawdust outfit was not going to produce a particularly convincing 'retail' Santa, but happy to come along for the free gift.

Then they would see Santa, the 'real' elves, the trees, the snow, the animals and you would see this look spread over their faces which said, "Oh right — bloody Nora - I am in the presence of the Great Gift Giver of the North, with all his remarkable powers of nocturnal high speed sleigh travel."

One particular incident has never left me and still fills me with shame, although I carry no blame for what happened.

A girl of probably eight year's old entered and froze on seeing that she had stumbled into an audience with his eminence the real Santa Clause, King of the North Pole.

At first she was terrified, then you could see her think, "OK well if this is the real guy then he is notoriously nice — he's the nicest guy of all — so I am completely safe." She visibly relaxed and approached, her mind now taken up with deciding what she *really* wanted for Christmas. After all this beauty could grant her any damned thing she wanted.

Jason Piette takes a turn as Santa with Charles (left) and John as the elves

I greeted her and introduced her to the elves who remained silent, then asked her what she wanted for Christmas.

She answered, with absolute conviction, in a very quiet, sweet, high pitched monotone voice.

"For Christmas I want the My Little Pony Grooming Parlour and ..."

She then took a deep breath and was about to add to her list when one of the elves let out a snort of laughter.

The problem was that the elves were not elves — they were nine year old boys. Nobody is as scornful of little girls as nine year old boys, particularly when they are revealing their deepest and fondest wish, and especially when that happens to be a livid pink grooming parlour for a ridiculous livid pink pony.

Although the first elf managed to cut his snort of laughter short the second elf now struggled, and failed, to control his own giggles. Of course he knew it was wrong and he tried as hard as

CHAPTER 17

he could to control that laughter. But this effort to control his laughter struck the first elf as funny, so that he too was now engaged in a monumental struggle to control his instincts to laugh his little half-rubberised face off. Then the pair of them lost it.

In the role of Santa Clause I felt the weight of responsibility on my shoulders. Although normally quick to laugh in serious situations, I was, in this case, the high priest, and rather than finding the situation funny I was horrified. I saw the little girl's eyes dart back and forth between the two giggling elves and the moment of hideous realisation that she was not in what, in modern parlance, might be called a 'safe space' but that even here, in Santa's holy of holies, her natural enemies, nine year old boys, had infiltrated, so that they could be cruel and mean.

I managed to cut the encounter short, gave her a gift and ushered her out.

I then, and I am not ashamed to admit it, beat up the elves.

Another incident occurred with Santa which might seem too grotesque to be real.

The thing about being Santa, which I now appreciate very well having done it, is that it is exhausting. The effort to be this otherworldly, delightful, charming, jovial, kind, loving character was a bit of a stretch. So although I was always initially happy to don the outfit and beard, after an hour or two it became a poisoned chalice. It was exhausting because there was a real sense of responsibility when interacting with the children. They believed in you and you could not let them down. You had to throw yourself into the part with total commitment. Having volatile, unstable elves didn't help.

The result of this was that any males knocking about would find themselves being asked to do a spell as Santa, and this included a friend of The Twins called Henry Kinross. By this point The Twins were older — probably about 16, and Henry happened to be large enough to be convincing, but he was actually quite a youngster. But what went wrong was not on account of his youth but due to his peanut allergy.

The gift shop at Christmas with an elf (Charles)

What Henry did not know was that the person who had been Santa prior to him had eaten a peanut butter sandwich *through* the beard. Whatever advice sufferers from this serious allergy are given, it is unlikely that they are told to beware of Santa beards through which peanut butter sarnies have passed. As Henry sat spreading bonhomie he began to feel a horrendous burning sensation on his lips and face. He tried to dismiss it as being merely the prickling of the beard but unfortunately, while children were still in attendance, the pain exploded, his face began to swell at an unprecedented rate and he was forced to tear the beard off, revealing a bloated, scarlet face, dripping with perspiration. The children's screams could be heard across the yard.

Whether you grow up in a council flat or a castle, Christmas should be a magical time for children, but to me it seemed that the farmhouse at Badsell was the ultimate perfect setting. Apart from anything else, whereas many children have to do an imaginative leap to believe that Santa could come down their chimney, if they even have one, the fireplace and chimney in the farmhouse at Badsell were so huge it seemed to have been built specifically to enable a fat man to clamber down it. There was even a strange little upstairs room with a tiny metal door that lead into the chimney at the first floor level, as though Santa had requested, at some point in history, that he be handed his mince pies at this particular juncture.

Our parents always put our Christmas stockings on our beds and they used these huge off-white woollen fisherman's socks for our gifts. Feeling the weight of this at the end of the bed, when it was still dark at dawn on Christmas morning, was and remains the most exciting sensation of all time. The socks were not big enough for larger gifts so there would always be a few extra things at the foot of the bed. We would take our stockings into Mum and Dad's room and remove and discuss the items one at a time.

As kids we attended the church in Paddock Wood on Christmas Day, a tradition that seems to have started with one of our more religious nannies, who started taking us to church regularly on Sundays, which included Sunday school.

The Church in Paddock wood (St Andrew's) was built in 1953 to replace the old church that was destroyed by a German bomb in 1940, so it is a modern church, lacking the charm of other local churches like the ones in Matfield and Brenchley - but we remained loyal to it throughout my upbringing.

My chief memory of Christmas Day in St Andrew's is somewhat disgraceful.

We were all kneeling in prayer and everyone started reciting the Lord's Prayer together.

Nearby a man started loudly mumbling nonsense. He wasn't saying the words of the prayer but making a sort of 'prayer-like noise'. It was clear that he was not all there — there is no acceptable modern phrase, but in those days we would say 'simple,' these days we might say, 'special'.

As a family we like to laugh and we have a heightened sense of comedy. The more serious the subject or situation, the more likely we are to find comedy in it. It's not regarded as an acceptable way to be now, but it is quite a good way of coping with life's tragedies and the darker side of existence — as long as nobody has their feelings hurt of course.

When the special person started mumbling I knew someone was going to crack up. It was inevitable. The mumbling was funny in its own right, but the pauses between the lines of the prayer set up a miniature sense of tension and anticipation, which was always rewarded by another burst of perfectly timed gibberish. It was a Rowan Atkinson comedy sketch happening in real life, in church.

Surprisingly it was my Mum who cracked first — which somehow made it even funnier, because it was so inappropriate. Many will judge her, but I love the fact that Mum was still so full of laughter, at an age when most people have lost the ability to get the giggles at all.

Pretty soon I was struggling hard to control myself. What I will say is that we knew it was wrong, and we fought very heard to get it in hand. My Uncle Anto was not amused. I glanced at him and he was frowning deeply. The years had fallen away and he was annoyed that his little sister (Mum) was being naughty and getting the giggles in Church. I am glad to say that we did get the laughter under control pretty fast and nobody outside the family noticed.

One of my abiding memories of Christmas is going out first thing on Christmas morning and feeding all the animals.

It always struck me that for animals, Christmas Day was like any other day which I found faintly sad. I was emerging from a house full of decorations and presents and great excitement to the muddy walks between pens where everything was business as usual. I would try and hand out a few extra treats but it was

CHAPTER 17

the ferrets who I really spoiled. I would give them a bowl of milk with an egg cracked in it, bits of bread and, in the centre, a plucked sparrow, caught by hand in the pet shed and despatched with a quick flick of the wrist. Now of course I feel bad about the sparrow.

The Christmas that is most indelibly etched on my memory was the Christmas of 1978 when I was 12.

In the days leading up to that particular Christmas I came up with the brilliant idea of getting drunk for the first time. I think I had seen a film called The Lost Weekend, about an alcoholic, and I thought that being drunk looked funny, grown-up and interesting.

We were having a big Christmas party in the farmhouse and the guest list included everyone we knew socially in the wider neighbourhood.

There was the usual building excitement whenever we entertained in the farmhouse. A massive, and unusually thorough hoovering would take place alongside a massive general tidy up.

The big speciality in the party eats department was of course chicken *vol au vents,* which Mum was particularly adept at and which were a favourite of mine. The party would be centred on the 'big drawing room' which was part of the extension completed in 1973, but all the downstairs rooms were used, with food in the old drawing room (the old hunting lodge) and drinks served in the hallway so guests could grab one on entering.

An antique table stood in the hallway and on this was placed wine glasses and some huge bottles of a very basic red wine (though not the wine we sold in the shop — we would not have inflicted that on our guests).

When nobody was looking, and before a single guest had arrived, I grabbed a glass, filled it to the top with red wine and took it into what we then called The Nursery, the room to the immediate left of the front door — later we called this room The Nelson Room when it displayed our Nelson pictures and memorabilia.

There I gulped the full glass of red wine down in one go, noted that it tasted horrible, then returned the glass and carried on helping everyone get the party ready.

The problem was that I had no idea how much you had to drink to get drunk, and that first glass, apart from tasting vile, seemed to have no effect.

So I went back, filled another glass, went to the nursery, knocked it back, and returned the glass to the hallway.

I do not know how many times I did this, but it must have been a few.

Christmas in the farmhouse. Foreground: Anto and Ruth Thornely. Background from left: John, Charles, Adam, Vanessa Watson, Emma, Simon

My last memory of the night itself is of the doorbell going as the very first guest arrived. I went to answer it and as I opened the door the world suddenly tilted wildly. It was as if the door handle was pulling me along and at the same time my head had

CHAPTER 17

become incredibly heavy. I could not even raise it enough to see who had arrived.

The next thing I remember is being in my parent's bathroom, my head being dunked repeatedly in cold water by my furious father who was yelling at me for being a 'bloody idiot!' I think at that point the party was still going on, but this was quite a lot later.

Relatively early on Christmas morning I awoke with a clanging headache and the worst nausea I had experienced up to that point in my life. I threw up copious amounts of almost neat red wine into a sick bowl before settling down, feeling like death.

I had looked forward to that Christmas especially because the big toy that year was the skateboard and I knew that I was being given one. At that age we always knew what our presents were because our parents 'hid' them in the big wardrobe in their bedroom. In the build up to Christmas it was unbearable temptation, as a child, to know where your presents were hidden. When our parents were out we all three used to go and look at them.

The first hint I got that I was in serious trouble was when I saw my older brother, Rupert, skateboarding backwards and forwards past the open door of the bedroom I had been put in. I do not think he was doing this deliberately to upset me — that was the longest stretch of corridor in the house. - but at that moment I realised, with horrible clarity, that for me, Christmas was cancelled.

I learned nothing the next day about what had happened the night before because I was in such deep disgrace that nobody would speak to me. In fact nobody, with one exception, would even enter the room where I had been placed. I was left with Radio One playing and I have the sad distinction of having heard Radio One's jaunty Christmas Day broadcast live in its entirety with a hangover from hell.

The one person who did visit me was Nan, my grandmother. She was such an adoring and innocent person that she refused to believe that drinking wine was the sole cause of my illness. She insisted that I must also have some sort of bug. She gave me my gift which was a melodica, a sort of mini piano that you blow into. I think she also brought me tea and toast in the evening.

I was finally allowed to rejoin the family downstairs for Boxing Day dinner but my parents were still furious with me and could barely bring themselves to speak to me.

Only much later did I learn that, when it was discovered that I was drunk very early during the party, I had been banished upstairs. However I had repeatedly come downstairs and joined the party — at one point stark naked. I had therefore been drunk and naked in front of everyone I knew in the neighbourhood.

Ruth Thornely or 'Nan'

After that I had to endure a retelling of this episode every day on Christmas Day for the rest of my childhood and on into my early teens, late teens and early twenties. It was a Christmas Day ritual, the story being told just as we all sat down for our big Christmas lunch. Someone would mention the 'famous

CHAPTER 17

Christmas party' and then someone would mention that I had got drunk and then the whole thing would be described in excruciating detail. I was generally quite good at the battle of wits conducted at those family meals, but I never had any ammunition to deal with this onslaught and I would have to just sit soaking up the shame. Only in my early twenties did I begin the fightback, managing to suggest that the 'shaming' of me, all those years, was itself shameful. It wasn't a bad angle and it sort of worked.

As for red wine - I couldn't bear the stuff for years — but I got there in the end.

One Christmas tradition which endured throughout our time at Badsell was that, on Boxing Day, Kath and Ernie would come over with Ken, Brian, and Steve. We would exchange presents and have a few drinks — then Kath would be persuaded to sit at the grand piano and suddenly we would all feel like we were in an East End pub. While Kath played in that very distinctive 'pub' style, Ernie would belt out songs such as 'Roll out the Barrel" and 'Maybe it's Because I'm a Londoner," in his crooning style. According to Brian he did this at every event they attended that involved a microphone — particularly family weddings. "Like all Dad's" says Brian, "he could be embarrassing".

CHAPTER 18
HEALTH AND SAFETY

The cereal crop harvest was always a high point in the year. The harvester would be working day and night and men would constantly arrive on tractors pulling trailers designed to take the corn which was pumped directly into the cargo bay through the unloader which swung out from the main body of the combine while the harvester continued its work in the field.

As kids we were left to interact with this process pretty much at will, only occasionally being told to stand back or get off. We learned which were the friendly drivers and would even clamber into the cargo bays and stand letting the corn shower down on our heads from the harvester as the whole shebang drove along through the field. The corn would get into our shoes, our pockets, our hair and our clothes.

Amongst the corn would be all sorts of insects of which the most notorious was the 'stink bug,' a green shield bug which blasted out a fowl smelling liquid if it was alarmed or squashed. There would also be earwigs, and soldier beetles which we were convinced would suck our blood because they were red.

CHAPTER 18

The combine harvester unloading in the Sloping Field

Once it arrived back at the big Atcost barn the corn would be unloaded and then a vicious-looking metal auger would pump it up, using a corkscrew mechanism, and dump it into wherever it was going to be stored. We would muck about in the corn, making sure we didn't get grabbed by the lethal screw pump but having fun playing chicken with it as the corn around it collapsed.

This was of, course, all completely insane, but it was long before the modern obsession with safety. Mark Lucas, who worked on the farm, recalls that in his childhood days around Horsmonden there was a hop farm where one of the high hop wires extended right across the River Tease, so it could be anchored on the other side. He and his friends used to try and cycle across it on a bicycle without tyres or inner tubes. They never achieved it, and they would fall in the river with the bike often landing on top of them. Their other favourite pastime was to get in a tin bath and sail it down to the weir.

'Health and Safety' was such an alien concept to us as a family that we were hostile and mocking of the very idea of it.

That said, some of the stuff that went on was off-the-scale bonkers. Rupert remembers smashing a light switch in a barn with a hammer as a little boy. He gave himself a huge electric shock, then realised he couldn't run to anyone because it was his own fault.

The Badsell bungee

We offered an early version a bungee jump on the farm which just involved people dropping from a crane. Today The Twins argue heatedly about which of them was the first to test this adrenalin ride but it seems that Charles went first. He was uninjured and gave the thumbs up — whereupon John had a go and was shocked to find that the end of the fall was extremely abrupt and the rope 'seemed to lack elasticity'. He felt one of his eyeballs very nearly come out and has never been quite the same since. However, out of two people, one was unaffected - so bungee jumping was added to Badsell's array of attractions .

CHAPTER 18

One of the worst injuries that occurred to a child was probably when a friend of The Twins, Chris Walter, was clambering onto the little trailer attached to the Honda three wheeler motorbike. Charles revved the machine up and pulled away, tearing a substantial amount of flesh away from Chris's shin. He was driven to Kent and Sussex Hospital where Chris's father insisted that the surgeon lacked sufficient experience. Finally someone who had actually done the operation before was found. The flesh of the shin had to be pulled hard to put it back in place.

The people most likely to be injured, it seemed, were visitors who came to stay or hang out with us children. They were encountering objects, equipment and situations that were new to them, whereas we were accustomed to all the dangers.

There was a French exchange student called Arnaud who my brother Rupert persuaded to have a go on the 'fire escape' while his parents were still having a drink with my parents in the living room at the very beginning of his stay.

Emma playing on the fire escape

The fire escape was a device that hung over my bed on the

third floor. In a fire you were meant to thread the big canvas loop under your arms and clamber out the window. A mechanism then lowered you to the ground.

Arnaud allowed the big loop to slip from under his arms and he went into free fall, breaking his arm. His planned stay of two weeks at Badsell shrank to about an hour, with the rest of his short stay in England spent in A&E.

An Australian boy also came a cropper while abseiling down using the same equipment — he put his feet through my parents bedroom window and cut his leg. Meanwhile we used this fire escape so often that it became positively mundane.

The fire escape wasn't used, however, when there was a serious fire. For a while Charles chose one of the attic rooms as his bedroom. It had been used by the family to store junk but recognising that it offered security from parental interference, being up the tall narrow third floor stairs, and behind a closable door, he selected it so that he could do all the things that pre-teens want to do unchallenged. The cause of the fire was something he calls an 'ashtray candle,' a semi-decorative freestanding multi purpose object.

The room had become headquarters to a loose gang consisting of The Twins, any visiting school friends, the Mead sisters, and other similarly aged teens then working on the farm. At some point someone chose to light the ashtray candle and then leave it flickering away on its own. As Charles recounts it, "I came back up to my room to find that everything was on fire, the bed, the carpet - the lot. Had I been a moment later it would have been too late and the house would have burned to the ground." As it was he was able to extinguish the flames and nobody outside his immediate circle, and certainly no adult, ever knew about it.

John once broke his collar bone when he came down the steep track that ran down the Old Orchard on his bike. The

CHAPTER 18

tricky thing was to sufficiently retain control of the speeding bicycle so that you could steer your way over the little bridge at the bottom. On this occasion he missed the bridge completely and shot into thin air instead, almost clearing the stream. The front wheel hit the far bank but the rest of the bike, and John, then went into the water. On another occasion The Twins engaged in a spear fight with sharpened bamboo canes. One of these went right through a hand.

For all the dangers that were laid out everywhere, ladders, rickety chairs, loose animals, heavy machinery, poisons, and so on, there was never an actual fatality to one of the customers. One child was hit by my older brother on his motorbike and had a tooth knocked out. A woman was once swinging on a rope swing over the pond half way up the sloping field in Solly's Wood when the rope snapped. All that happened, according to her, was that she fell in the pond and lost her 'distress whistle', which was admittedly unfortunate because, at that moment, she needed it.

A man once came to the door and angrily complained to my father that a chair he had been seated on had collapsed like matchwood. The man had brought his own picnic, which we did not allow, and they were eating on our lawn after Badsell had closed to the public for the day after a very busy weekend. My father said to him, with great menace "If you leave now, I wont make you pay for the damage." His simmering rage terrified the man who left immediately.

The closest we ever came to a customer death was due to the ball pond in the play barn. It was an inflatable dome filled with thousands of coloured plastic balls.

At the end of the day, when the public were gone, Nick Belton and The Twins would get in there and fling the balls at each other hard. Then they would take it in turns to switch the air pump off, climb onto it, and then blow it up again, so that it would fling you off (Nick got his first black eye doing this.)

One day someone switched it off and it collapsed completely with a child still inside. When he was finally dragged out he had turned blue. This incident was so serious that even my parents recognised that things needed to improve. Generally, though, our attitude to 'health and safety' was that it was joy-killing bureaucrats protecting their own backs.

Rupert and Adam tree climbing in 1972

I have no doubt that many hideous accidents happened on farms during the sixties and seventies and that is why the Health and Safety Executive had to step in and change the culture. We, however, got nothing but joy from all this freedom and we learned to take calculated risks, to figure out for ourselves how far you could take things. By the end of my childhood I could climb pretty much any tree and I would go incredibly high.

Needless to say we were not very politically correct in those days and many of the things that made us laugh, at the end of a hard day, when we were sitting around the kitchen table

CHAPTER 18

drinking and smoking, are things that you cannot laugh about now.

One incident involving a member of the staff who had a stutter springs to mind.

On Saturday afternoons, if everything was running smoothly on the farm, my father might retreat to the farmhouse for a break, but of course any crisis would lead to the front door buzzer going.

One time a member of the staff, who usually worked in the shop, came to the door which was opened by my father.

"S-s-s-someone's sh-sh-sh-shut themselves in the toilet," he was told.

My Dad had a simple solution for that and offered to get a hammer. But no, he was told, they had not 'shut' themselves, they had 'sh-sh-sh-sh-shot' themselves. This was much more serious and Dad's face expressed great anguish. "Are you sure they've shot themselves?" he asked.

"No not shot themselves — sh-sh-sh-sh-shat themselves."

It emerged that the man in question needed my father to lend him a pair of trousers.

As my Dad puts it all these year's later "I told him I did not want the trousers back."

CHAPTER 19
A MAGNET FOR ALTERNATIVE PEOPLE

If there is one thing that characterised my childhood at Badsell it was that there were always people visiting, coming to stay, coming to work, coming for dinner, coming to chat. Amongst the farming fraternity you never really called people and said you were coming — you just turned up at G&T time.

There was little distinction between who was a friend and who was an employee. On one occasion Mum hired a very strong and highly independent character, still a friend today, called Rosie Cornwallis, to work in the pet enclosure. Rosie was simply too strong willed to work for anyone. Gail Belton recalls her ticking off a child rather forcefully for picking up a rabbit. Mum said something along the lines of, "Look, Rosie forget working for me — you're fired — but come and have a drink and let's be friends instead."

One of the striking things about those Badsell days was the number of people who worked there. In many cases they saw the place as a home-from-home and quite a few lived there — either in caravans, in the upstairs of the oast or in the farmhouse itself.

CHAPTER 19

In fact some friends lived in the farmhouse for years, often coming for a long weekend then getting lured into working on the farm. They had a warm bed, great food and paid work but I think a huge part of the attraction was the chance to be part of a warm family circle and a lively social scene. Mum used to tell me about someone who lived in her household when she was growing up - although it was slightly different.

My grandfather Frank Thornely grew up in a grand country house called Eyton Hall near Leominster with multiple servants, one of whom, Florence Culley, came to work for Frank's family aged 14. Always known as Florrie, she eventually came back to live with Frank and Ruth Thornely and the children when she became a widow in the 1940's. She moved with them to Peynetts in Goudhurst where she got by on her tiny pension, preferring to be part of a family than living alone in poverty. As Nick Thornely recalls it, 'she seemed to be the only person with cash, you could always borrow money off Florrie'. When Ruth became a widow and moved to Little Fish Hall, Florrie again moved with her and it was there she ended her days.

At Badsell we didn't just have people living in the farmhouse. The huge space above the gift shop, which had been our roller skating arena as children, became a storage space for one of Dad's old employers, Dewe Rogerson. When someone from the company arrived to search for some documents they found Australian students had made beds out of the stacks of papers and old advertising posters.

Two ex-soldiers from Scotland even lived in the stables for a while, both survivors of the Enniskillen bomb. There was a tall one called Sid and a short one whose name has been forgotten. They just turned up and were given a job putting up fencing in the pet area. They were hard characters and later one of them ended up in prison. He wrote to Dad from his cell and Dad replied, but after a while he got a reply back saying, "Thanks Simon but I can't for the life of me read your dreadful handwriting."

In Charles' memory the two Scotsmen were 'escaped convicts' who were on the run and came to Badsell to lie low. One night a fox got into one of the chicken houses, with tragic consequences. Knowing that a fox often returns the following night, Charles offered to stay up with the shotgun. Dad agreed but only on the condition that an adult stay up with him. In Charles' words "It was decided that one of the escaped convicts would stay up with me, to ensure my safety." When it came to it the fox did return, and Charles was about to shoot it when the Scotsman trained a torch on it.

Like my Uncle Ben before him, my cousin Sam Thornely came to live at the farm for a while in 1987, after he had finished school, in order to work and save up for his year-off trip to Africa.

He had just passed his driving test and he drove across from Thornbury near Bristol in his vintage 2CV — a journey which felt at the time like an epic voyage.

By his own admission, years at private school had left him with few practical skills, and like almost everyone else he had a near-fatal accident while driving the three wheeler Honda motorbike. He was driving around the farm with the shotgun, when he came across a fox and decided to give chase. He went down a bank and the whole thing rolled over him while he was holding a loaded shotgun with the safety catch off. Luckily the trike just bounced over him.

Sam loved learning new skills, such a ploughing or connecting the Massey Fergusson up to some piece of equipment. Eventually he did start to get more practical and the experience built his confidence. Meanwhile he was often teamed up with Mark Lucas, an extremely practical man who took the piss

CHAPTER 19

out of Sam endlessly. As Sam remembers it, Mark was always saying, "What you done now Sam?" following the latest mishap.

He remembers Mark as a great storyteller. They would be driving along together in the van and Mark would point to a house. "I once crashed my motorbike right into that house " he'd say, "I ended up in their living room."

Mark Lucas in the farmhouse kitchen

As well as working on the farm, Sam was a general dogsbody, dropping Dad off at Paddock Wood station and The Twins off at school in Tonbridge every morning. He remembers it as a great time. It was the harvest, a gorgeous autumn, and it left him with a lifetime love of the countryside. Years later he bailed out of the rat race in London and went to live in a tipi in a forest in Dumfries and Galloway. Mum sent him bags of seeds and he created a vegetable patch.

It wasn't just Mark who took the piss out of Sam - he remembers the strawberry pickers teasing him remorselessly — referring to him as their 'toy boy' when he was trying to be taken seriously as overseer. The piss taking went up another notch when he managed to turn over the trailer on the Honda three-wheeler when it was loaded with full strawberry trays.

The other major cock up Sam recalls is when he was sent to drill the big sloping field with corn. Mark and Mum urged him to make sure the seed didn't run out. Sure enough he forgot to check it and spent about an hour drilling nothing into the earth. He then had to try and find the point at which the corn had run out — which he failed to do. He remembers poor Mum and Mark, both exhausted after a busy day, on their hands and knees in the field trying to identify the point at which they needed to start drilling seed again.

Mark Lucas was very much a part of Badsell as was Andy Browning.

They had a building company called Quad construction which was named after their four wheel drive Canadian Ford gun tug, a relic from the Second World War which had a crane device on the back and ran 50 miles to the gallon on cheap 'red' diesel.

Quad Construction's Canadian Ford gun tug in the Badsell yard.

Andy and Mark first appeared when Mum needed build-

CHAPTER 19

ings for the rare breeds park. They became part of the fabric of the farm for the next twenty years or so. They did all the work converting the large oast house into a shop and café and started storing their equipment and materials down the valley in a series of buildings they put up themselves and which, much later, were converted into a home for Sandy and John Schofield. Their work on other farms often involved dismantling buildings and these ended up being stored down the valley at Badsell. Then, when Mum said she needed a shed put up, they were given a new life on the farm.

Andy and Mark fitted in because they had the 'Badsell attitude.' Everything was possible as long as you weren't aiming for perfection. They understood how to keep costs down and that you didn't always have to buy everything brand new. Just as importantly, they were good company, good storytellers, and they enjoyed a party.

Andy Brownings father, Ray, was a farmer. Born in East Dulwich, his family ran one of the first transport cafés, The Walnut. As a youngster he worked with his identical twin brother Morris (always known as Moggy) in London at The Embassy club and The Savoy, pocketing huge tips as bellboys. In the war he was in the Royal Observer Corp , spotting aircraft. For a while he was a butler to Lord and Lady Reading but at some point during the war he moved down to work on a farm with his father and his brother. He and his twin attempted to get into the RAF but were turned down. Ray had become a skilled cowman and shepherd and had to stay working the land while Moggy got into the Paratroopers. Accidentally dropped behind enemy lines in Burma, Moggy spent the rest of the war in a Japanese prison camp. He lost six stone but survived.

Andy was born at Etchingham and from the age of seven he grew up on a substantial farm called Little Tottingworth owned by his uncle at Broad Oak near Heathfield. Andy lived at Old

Tottingworth in the converted laundry of what had once been the substantial estate of Sir Harry Oaks. Andy's bedroom in the loft of the old laundry was enormous, 28 feet by 14 feet, though he shared it with two brothers.

Andy Browning in the yard at Badsell

At Little Tottingworth they had up to three hundred cattle as well as pigs and sheep. They grew cereal crops and even had their own mill for turning the grain into animal feed. At some point Andy's father fell out of the top of a barn while loading hay. This left him with a curvature of the spine and he had to give up farm work. A film producer called Kenneth Shipman then hired him and his wife Irene at their house close to Tottingworth, building them a bungalow to live in. As a child Andy sometimes glimpsed Hollywood glamour when Kenneth had parties and remembers seeing the Kojak actor, Telly Savalas at a party (Kojac, for small boys in the 1970s, was a very big deal.)

Andy was dyslexic and he had a hard time at school. At primary school he was bullied and, as he puts it, "At secondary school I was bullied by the teachers." If he turned up he got beaten so he stopped going.

His first job was assistant gamekeeper at Wadhurst Park. He then worked on the family farm for a while but "working for family doesn't work — there's no overtime!" He then worked on the next farm along doing logging for pulpwood — very hard

CHAPTER 19

physical labour. A building boom lured him into the building trade and he did things like hod carrying, before eventually teaming up with Mark Lucas.

Andy describes Badsell as "a magnet for alternative people. It wasn't always clear how people found the place but people just turned up and ended up working there and they were very rarely everyday people".

Andy's farming background and experience with animals meant that he got more and more involved with Badsell as time went on.

Mark was born and grew up in Horsmonden where his father, Jack, worked at Lambert's, operating steam engines. He ended up owning a famous Royal Chester engine which had been used as the model for a miniature. For a while he kept this huge engine outside his house on Gibbet Lane in Horsmonden.

Steam engines and workers at Lamberts, Horsmonden. The tall man near the centre with his hands on his hips is Mark Lucas' father Jack

Mark spent a lot of his childhood on fruit farms around Horsmonden and went to the village school before going on to Mascalls in Paddock Wood (now Mascalls Academy). His first job was with Atcost Barns who were responsible for the big barn at Badsell. They used to set off from Atcost in Paddock Wood, towing a DeLorean caravan which they would live in while they erected barns on farms around the country. Wherever they were their wage packets would be waiting for them at the nearest Post Office on Thursday morning.

After a stint of two or three years in Australia, Mark married and settled into a life in the building trade and at some point he teamed up with Andy Browning and they started putting up steel buildings.

Andy and Mark were a double act, and they put me in mind of Laurel and Hardy, with Andy being lanky and skinny, while Mark was a big bear of a man. Certainly a lot of their stories seemed to involve comical near-disasters but to suggest that they were clumsy and inept would be unfair. The fact was that if they put up a building without any incidents then it did not merit a story — but if something untoward happened it became a well polished gem.

On one occasion they were working on a ninety foot tall corn silo on a farm near Leatherhead. Mark went up the built-in ladder on the side to open the hatch at the top and then climbed down again — at which point the entire ladder, being rotten, completely collapsed.

Another time Andy and Mark were asked to discretely take down a huge shed and replace it with an Atcost barn. Discretion was required because no planning permission had been sought. While dismantling the huge shed it started to collapse on top of Andy and he shimmied up a ladder to escape being crushed. The ladder then catapulted him and he landed on his head on concrete. The sheer noise of the collapse ensured that 'discretion' was thrown out the window and as Mark puts it "every fence had a person looking over it."

This incident happened near Marden and 'discretion' became even more abandoned when a helicopter was sent to airlift Andy to hospital, requiring several horses to be moved out of an adjacent field. As Andy was being loaded into the helicopter his dog, Moss, bit one of the medics.

CHAPTER 19

On yet another occasion they put up a scaffolding tower to work on a building near Leeds Castle. The farmer arrived with a company rep and a couple of other people and they stood watching them work. Andy was at the very top of the scaffolding tower when something went catastrophically wrong and the whole thing collapsed in slow motion, lowering Andy to the ground standing upright. When he reached the bottom he stepped off with a flourish and shouted "tada!" as though it was all a deliberate stunt.

Andy definitely seemed to have a guardian angel. As he puts it "I am the only person I know who has driven a Ford Escort *through* a telegraph pole." This incident took place during the 'Badsell years'.

He crashed his car on Half Moon Lane, turning it over in the process, when he had imbibed enough booze to ensure that he would lose his licence if he was breathalysed.

His friends the Meads leaped into action, dragged him out of the vehicle and taking him back to Dislingbury, where they lived. There they hid him in the attic and plied him with brandy so they could claim, when the police arrived, that he had drunk since the accident, to calm his nerves.

Meanwhile Andy's son, Ben, called Tony Long at Paddock Wood Motors. When the police arrived Tony was half way through dragging the car off the road. By this time there were quite a few people at the scene who all started to tell the police different stories about what had happened to the driver. The police didn't find Andy until about 3 a.m.

They threw the book at him, ignoring all the pleading about drinking brandy after the accident and all the other Byzantine stories that were swirling around. However when the case came to Tunbridge Wells Magistrates court Andy's barrister noticed that nobody had actually asked Andy if he was driving the vehicle in question and the case was thrown out. About ten days later he received a cheque for all his legal expenses.

When Andy moved on to work at Baker Construction, Mark worked for a while with my brother Rupert, still putting up barns, but they also got involved with buying and sandblasting old telephone boxes when they were being sold off in the 1980s. One of these ended up on the front lawn at Badsell for several years, until it was run over on the 'Andean Day'. Sandblasting became a bit of a speciality for them.

Rupert's wife Samantha made her very first visit to Badsell by train. She had imagined a romantic encounter with him when he collected her at Paddock Wood Station but instead was met by 'Nan' who demanded to know: 'How did you meet our son and heir?" She then explained that Rupert was too busy sandblasting to come himself.

When Mark and Rupert were working together they were occasionally hired by Mum to do work on the farm and one time, when part of the oast house was being turned into the café, she decided to move the diesel tank from on top of the gantry. She had two ornamental pheasants living in an enclosure under the gantry so these had to be moved.

They opened the door and the magnificent Reeves Pheasant flew over Mark's shoulders and ended up on the hedge between Ernie Wiseman and Joyce Miles' gardens. After a very prolonged hunt they managed to retrieve the bird and put it in its new quarters, but when they went back to get a rare albino pheasant, it dropped dead from shock.

They propped the bird up in a wicker cage in the farmhouse kitchen. Mark found a business card for a taxidermists and inserted it in the beak. While having a gin and tonic after work Mark told Mum "I think that bird is trying to tell you something".

Andy and Mark were never working full time at Badsell but

CHAPTER 19

when things were quiet on the construction side there was always something that needed doing on the farm. Whatever job they were doing at Badsell would be interrupted by the need to move pigs, dip sheep, or some other task involving the many animals in the pet area.

Mark Lucas on the Honda three-wheeler with Nick Belton

Mark was, and remains, a great story teller who seems to occupy a universe where absurd things happen all the time. He recently reminded me about a man who haled from Wales who kept a shire horse for a while on the farm, and offered punters rides. One day he said, with complete confidence to Mark, "One thing you'll never see my son, you'll never see a horse die in front of you, it will always go off and die on its own." The next morning he was again standing with Mark by the field. He went up to the gate and went, "Hello, my lovely." The horse turned around and dropped dead.

Sitting in the Badsell farmhouse kitchen after a day's work, Mark would tell shocking and fascinating stories of his time working on military bases and aircraft hangers in Libya, prior to the US airstrikes in 1986. Much of the raw material for this work had been 'hidden' by the Americans by burying it in the desert, so each project began with workers digging it all up again.

Mark and his fellow British workers used to brew their own hooch in the wardrobes in their rooms, using grape juice, yeast and sugar. One perk of working on top secret military installations was that they had access to Colonel Gaddafi's own Mercedes lorry which was rigged up with powerful Siemen's satellite telephones. Normally it was impossible to call home but Mark and his mates would sneak into the lorry and call home direct. They always had a screwdriver in their hand so if anyone caught them they could pretend to be mending it.

Mark once witnessed a man nick the back of a sheep leg with a knife then insert a rubber tube into the wound connected to an air pump. The pressure peeled the animal's skin away from its flesh, and it was then skinned alive right in front of him. I was deeply shocked by the cruelty of this when he told me.

William McInally with Tamworth piglets

Badsell was an important place for William McInally who was born in 1971 and grew up in Biggenden Farmhouse on

CHAPTER 19

Waterman's Lane near Paddock Wood with five sisters and four brothers — most of them, like him, being fostered. He began working at Badsell in 1989 while studying horticulture and agriculture at Hadlow College. Initially it was a Saturday job but he ended up working full time through a scheme run by the government called Remploy. At first he would cycle to the farm on a mountain bike but later he got himself a moped. Today William lives in Glasgow, he has four grownup children, and is a grandad. He also has two cats and two gerbils. He remembers his Badsell days with great fondness and keeps in touch with some of the people he worked with.

Whenever there was any sort of problem with electricity at Badsell, which was often, we called a tall skinny man called Ivan Rumary with wild frizzy hair. The rumour was he had received so many electric shocks that he carried a permanent electric charge — The Twins still claim today that if he put a light bulb in his mouth it lit up. My sister Emma claims he only had to put the bulb on top of his head, like a lamp.

In fact Ivan worked in the day as a heating engineer and doing property maintenance. He had known some of the other people who worked on the farm for years - Gail and Bob Belton and Mark Lucas, and they had all been motorcycle enthusiasts in their twenties, meeting up in Horsmonden when the village had three pubs (The Gun, The Townhouse and The Kings Arms).

Ivan completed his 'City and Guilds' after periods studying at West Kent College, Maidstone and Brighton College, all during the period when the old Imperial measuring systems were going over to Metric - meaning he had to do two sets of exams. As he puts it 'they taught us everything in those days' so he learned to do plumbing, electricity, heating equipment, the works.

He first came to Badsell when Mark Lucas recommended

him to my Dad to fix an electricity fault. Later Ivan and his wife Sally became part of the Badsell 'circle,' attending many of the events there. At one point he was instructed by Mum to install central heating in the mouse house, which he did using a hairdryer, although it soon burned out. Ivan even got involved in a scheme, possibly dreamed up by Dad, to clear out the pond in Solly's Wood half way up the sloping field to create a fishing lake. Work began with a digger but then a man called Hobbs appeared. According to Mark Lucas this man had been alerted by his wife, who was a strawberry picker. He arrived clutching a copy of the ancient Ordinance Survey map, on which Badsell was called "Bog Hole," and announced that work had to stop because the pond was an 'archeological site'. Certainly that part of the farm is dotted with these immense holes which are likely to be connected with Iron Age.

If electricity issues came up Ivan always came to the farm in the evening and would inevitably end up seated at the kitchen table, smoking his roll-ups and telling stories. Speaking to him recently I discovered that Ivan, possibly as part of the scheme to create fishing lakes on the farm, was responsible for stocking the pond at the end of the drive with carp. He drove to Rochester and bought a bag of baby carp which he released into the pond by the end of the drive. This happened about thirty years ago but my daughter and I were kindly given permission to fish in the pond by Sandy and John Schofield recently. We spent many hours trying to catch a large and very distinctive blue-black carp that is so canny it swallowed our bait several times then spat it out. At one point I actually caught it but it seemed to untie the hook inside its mouth, leaving me with an end of gnarly line.

We became so determined to catch this fish that we camped out over the night but in the morning we were poised to give up altogether when Tabby hooked a young carp, just a few inches long. As the morning progressed we started pulling in a whole

CHAPTER 19

series of modestly sized fish, all no-doubt descendants of the carp Ivan released thirty odd years back. We released them back of course, "and Away!"

Ivan now lives in Norfolk and remembers the Badsell days fondly. He is honest enough to admit to a bit of piss taking of William McInally. He recalls being with Trevor Ralph on the farm when William came over and said that the mower was broken. The two men took a look at it and advised William to replace the spark plug. William cycled off to Paddock Wood and returned with the new spark plug. The machine still did not work and he again asked them for help.

They took another look at it and asked him if he had remembered to get 'a box of sparks' to go with the plug. When he shook his head they sent him again to Paddock Wood to buy them. What happened when William asked for a box of sparks in Paddock Wood Motorist Centre is not recorded.

There were several families who worked on the farm. In addition to the Beltons there were also the Pipers - Joan and her sons Colin and Nigel and daughter Julie. We never quite got over the fact that the father's name was Maurice Piper.

Another important family were the Meads. Their connection to Badsell began because Nico Mead was friends with Sarah Long with whom she attended Mascalls School in Paddock Wood. Sarah was already working at the farm and in 1992, Nico began working in the shop and the petting area, aged 13, on Saturdays and Sundays and in the school holidays. Later her sister Carly came and worked in the café.

Nico remembers The Twins coming home from Tonbridge School on the weekends and "strolling around with Jesse the dog, looking very important and quite terrifying".

Both Carlie and Nico became good friends with The Twins, as they still are today. At one point their mother, Angie, came and asked Mum if she could leave her pony Briar there for

Christmas. Briar never left and by the end the Meads had 13 ponies and horses living at Badsell, from Shetlands to a heavy horse called Lady Elena, in various fields and enclosures. Some were kept in what Nico remembers being called 'The Naughty Yard' down the valley by the collection of buildings put up by Andy and Mark.

Angie had had a rural horsey upbringing and she eventually persuaded Mum that the farm needed to offer heavy horse and cart rides. Her husband, Spencer, was an extremely skilled carpenter who worked on film and commercial sets all over the word and he built the cart. To pay for all her horses living and grazing at Badsell many of Angie's horses were also used for pony rides.

The Mead children had a very unusual Bohemian childhood, travelling with the Footsbarn Theatre and this may be why they felt so at home at Badsell, a place with a somewhat Bohemian character.

Nico has really happy memories of Badsell because it was, "Just freedom, really. And it felt like a community made up of little tribes." These tribes overlapped and Nico felt like part of several of them, such as our family, those working on the farm, and the worker's kids. Another gang was "Ben Browning and the naughty boys at the back". Ben was car mad and today he repairs them at Paddock Wood Motors. As a youngster at Badsell he would do up old bangers and as Nico puts it "We used to tear across the fields in them."

Badsell was soon a centre of Nico and Carly's social life and as teenagers, after a rave or just an informal hangout, they would find a place to sleep next to the pig stye in the pet area office, or in the farmhouse. Nico recalls being first up and my father handing her the Sunday Times supplement and a boiled egg.

Nico also has happy memories of the hunter trials at

CHAPTER 19

Badsell. A proper course was built with huge solid cross country jumps dotted along a route that took you right around the farm. Nico would ride her mother's pony, Sandy, a "terrifying pony". The course included a water jump that involved landing in the stream by the end of the Blackberry Field. Nico describes it as "the most incredible ride imaginable, tearing around the land on a horse was just heaven," but , she adds, "I always fell off!"

Sophie Denny became a big part of the farm for a while, living in the farmhouse while working in the pet area. She formed a very close bond with a piglet called Mouse that had been rejected by its mother, keeping it warm by carrying it everywhere in her bra. Mouse even got some press coverage, possibly because the British press always liked any story that gave them an excuse to focus on a woman's 'chest'!

Sophie Denny and 'Mouse' as they appeared in a newspaper

For several people Badsell became a sort of home from home, with Mum acting almost as a surrogate mother, or mother figure, just as her mother Ruth had done at Paynetts in Goudhurst.

Nick Sergeant recalls the 'dawn 'till (after) dusk lifestyle' fondly. He sent me a list to sum up his memories of Badsell, boiling it all down to the essentials:

- Hut
- Barn
- Camp
- Cheese melts
- Being put to work by Celia
- Numerous personal injuries
- Numerous (witnessed) injuries of others
- Thrown off hay bales (20/30ft)
- Shot in the foot
- Crashing cars
- Raiding houses
- The "poison shed"
- Walks to Dovecote / Matfield for solid underage drinking
- School Leaving party @ 12yrs old, all night + booze
- Bunny basher

Badsell was an important place for Jessica Kopiski (now Taplin) who describes it as a 'sanctuary of smiles & kindness, ribaldry with the best intent, sunshine and black tie parties off the back of tractors.' For her my parents lay at the beating heart of it all and she describes how Mum's wisdom, friendship and maternal kindness set her life back on track and made her 'a better version of me'. "I owe her so much" she says, and concludes:."What splendid memories of moments that have made me a wiser and happier mother and person."

For the last part of our time at Badsell we had a chef who lived in a caravan on the farm. He was an ex-navy caterer and one night my parents awoke to find him throwing stones at their window and shouting that there was a fire. My father alleges that he was drunk and shouting, "She's ablaze from stem to stern Captain," although this seems a bit far fetched. Two fire engines arrived but there was no fire and the story goes that the chef (allegedly) had been trying to get his hands on the keys to the oast house so that he could get at the wine. This has never been

CHAPTER 19

proven. The firemen were, as usual, given beers for their trouble.

Another character was always known as "The Leather Man," though he was actually called Derek. He made things out of leather in one of the sheds and sold them in the farm shop. He managed to get his hands on an early photocopier which, as Mark Lucas remembers, was the size of a piano and ran on coal dust. He was always trying to get people to use his photocopier, which stood for a while in the roundel of the oast. Mark remembers getting an enthusiastic lecture about the photocopier while he could see, over Derek's shoulder, my Mum gesturing to indicate that the man was insane.

'The Fish Lady' used to give demonstrations of fly fishing on the lawn and sold fresh trout. Just a few days after her husband died Dad got a call from her. "I wonder if you'd like to come and have a look at his clothes," she told him, "he's left a lot of smart clothes which I am selling. I won't be needing them."

A dutch girl called Marion stayed on the farm for a summer season and endlessly played the 'Birdy Song' on an accordion.

Kevin Walsh came to Badsell as a young boy and helped out in the farm shop for about three years when it was in the roundel of the oast, spending most of his weekends and summer holidays and even sometimes coming after school. At the age of 14, Dad taught him to drive in the blue Range Rover and he remembers going with him to tie cardboard signs advertising PYO strawberries to the trees on Crittenden Road. He has since enjoyed a varied career in show business. In his early twenties he was a corporate Party DJ and he became a game show host presenter for breweries and outside events for Radio 210fm. For over twenty years he hosted events in West End bars and production companies used to come searching for talent at his "Backing the Stars" nights. He has performed at the London Palladium and these days he does one hour spots as a singer and entertainer in care homes, lunch clubs and day centres.

A publicity image taken for a hog roast at Badsell. Back row from left: Ben Browning, Donny Kent, Nick Belton, Paul Barden, front row: Gail Belton, Sophie Denny and Marion (a seasonal worker from Holland)

Paul was a ruddy cheeked young man who, like so many people who ended up working on the farm, just turned up at the front door one day. He was carrying a few tools and asked Mum if there was any gardening work. Mum was inclined to welcome anyone who took the trouble to travel to the farm and instantly warmed to anyone with an interest in gardening. He was hired on the spot.

He was also carrying a bible and was an evangelical Christian in a world that was not just lacking in piety but was often downright pagan. It meant that he came occasionally into conflict with other members of staff, or to put it in plain English, everyone took the piss out of him.

He soon learned to largely keep his beliefs to himself but there was one opportunity to proselytise uninterrupted.

One of the popular activities for visitors was to go for a tractor ride. For this a special trailer had been built by Mark Lucas with bench seating and caged sides in case the whole thing rolled over. Ernie Wiseman called these tractor rides 'The

CHAPTER 19

Sex Tour' because they would often encounter couples frolicking in the long grass. Paul was often in the driver's seat and he would take punters right down to The Sewer Field and high up to the top of the sloping field where they enjoyed unimpeded views of the Kent countryside.

We did not know that he was also giving sermons until we gave one of many raves in the big barn. On this occasion the party had been fancy dress and one reveller, John, had gone as King Henry VIII. He had not actually gone to bed at all. Instead, when the time had come for him to take his rest, he had simply walked off into the countryside. He had finally fallen asleep face down in the sewer field, wrongly assuming he would not be disturbed, with his crown still on his head but at a jaunty angle.

Paul was aware of the ungodly and sinful bacchanalia that had taken over the farm the night before and, it being Sunday, was at his most evangelical. He arrived at the sewer field on the tractor, pulling the trailer full of unsuspecting visitors, who, at most, were hoping to see a squirrel.

Paul set eyes on the unconscious Henry VIII and decided that this was the perfect opportunity to teach a valuable lesson. He parked up beside the unconscious John, stood up high on the back of the tractor and raised a finger into the air.

'Here before you lies a sinner!" He allegedly yelled. "One who has strayed from the path of righteousness and fallen into the arms of the devil." As he went on John awoke and became aware of what was happening, but did not dare move his body for fear that the motion would cause him to vomit. And so it was that he had to take his deserved punishment from the mouth of one of God's own people.

GOODBYE BADSELL

A picture featuring many of the people who worked, lived or hung out at Badsell in the 1990s. Back row: 2 unknown men, 2nd row (standing) from left: Celia Preston, Paul Barden, Nigel Hodges, William McInally, Unknown, Donny Kent, Janet the Candle,, Marion, Unknown, Mark Lucas, Simon Preston, Andy Browning with Rupert Mead on his shoulders, John Preston, Chris Walter, Vicky Long, Nico Mead, Carlie Mead, Sarah Long, Charles Preston, Seated (from left): Sharon Wiseman, Jane Fuller, Kath Wiseman, Christine Greaves, Sophie Denny, Gail Belton, Angie Mead, Seated on the ground (from left): Sean Wiseman, Kate Fuller, Nick Belton, Carl Browning, Georgie Belton (with the dog Custard), Ben Browning Photo: Elizabeth Kirkor Rogers

CHAPTER 20
DEFROSTING PETS

My parents were always trying to find new ways to earn money on the farm because, despite the fact that the place was a constant hive of activity and appeared to be a dizzying success, with 50,000 punters visiting a year, they were always slipping more and more into debt - a debt which eventually led to the enforced sale of the farm.

An example of the kind of thing they came up with was allowing a man called Terry Chapel to dump hardcore in an area down the valley next to the sewer field. Lorry after lorry used to go tearing down the valley - there was so much he actually paid to reinforced the track. The result for a while was a scene of such devastation, with huge piles of crushed concrete and sections of shattered walls and floors, that while working at Transatlantic Films in London, I used it as a location to film a sequence showing the aftermath of a war. This was for a series we were making for Channel 4 called Greek Fire. None of the footage was used because it was regarded as 'too extreme'.

Charles playing the part of a victim of war in the rubble in the Sewer Field

For a while we were getting groups of Japanese tourists visiting the farm and they would pay extra for a guided tour of the farmhouse.

The truth is it would be impossible to list all the many entrepreneurial enterprises that were running concurrently on the farm, not even the family knew about all of them. One Christmas a man came to the farmhouse door to buy a Christmas turkey. He was met by my uncle Anto who informed him, with total conviction, that providing plump Christmas turkeys was one thing we definitely did not do. In fact we had started selling frozen turkeys and my Dad was furious at the lost sale.

One day someone came up with the idea of running a pet cemetery on the farm. We had ample land, we were accustomed to dealing with deceased creatures but more importantly, as animal lovers, we were sympathetic to people who were grieving over a deceased pet.

Appropriately enough a lady called Christine Greaves had the original idea and she and her husband became partners in the enterprise.

It was called The Orchard Pet Cemetery and an area of the little orchard on the right as you came up the drive was selected to be the cemetery. One of the best things about the business

CHAPTER 20

was the logo they came up with - it featured an apple tree but you could clearly make out the shapes of animals in the gaps between the leaves.

Japanese tourists visiting Badsell in the 1990s

The cemetery business was run in classic Preston fashion. We dived into it with little investment and less knowledge, made it up as we went along and yet there was something charming and special about it.

Mum was brilliant with the customers who were often grieving as deeply as someone who had lost a child. I remember going to a house in Five Oak Green with Mum to collect a dead Alsatian. We were shown into the house and were confronted by a youngish woman with long dark hair kneeling on the floor, leaning forward over the corpse of an obese Alsatian.

The woman's long dark hair was hanging straight down and she looked like something out of a National Theatre production of The Trojan Women.

It was essential to be extremely sensitive and respectful in these situations but when it came to moving the actual animal we were soon grunting and groaning like a couple of builders shifting a steel girder. The thing weighed a ton. In fact overweight pets were a recurring theme. We were often dealing with pets that were so loved that their owners couldn't bare to deny them anything.

The funerals were always very solemn occasions and there was a general nervousness that our family's inclination to laugh in serious situations would shatter the funereal atmosphere and cause a scandal.

The Orchard Pet Cemetery logo

A story sprang up that at one dog funeral the client asked for a piece of classical music to be played and that The Twins were put in charge of providing this music. The story goes that they recorded the required piece on the 'B' side of a tape that had 'The Laughing Policeman', a 1926 recording by Charles Penrose, on the 'A' side. This song features a man laughing his head off and The Twins are supposed to have accidentally played an extended snatch of the song during the funeral. The story has been told so often it might as well be true.

One thing I was concerned about was that the coffins were lowered into the graves on ropes but there was nothing to stop the ropes from slipping sideways - there were no batons glued to the underside. In my usual role as 'Casandra' I pointed out to

CHAPTER 20

Mum that this was an accident waiting to happen but she just reassured me that this was not an issue.

A deceased dog ready for a customer visit before the funeral

Up to that point I had not actually been involved in a funeral but the next thing I knew I was being called in to assist at the burial of a much adored boxer dog.

Quite a large family group was gathered by the graveside, all in black, with Mum reading a poem ('The Power of a Dog' by Rudyard Kipling.)

The moment came for the coffin to be lowered.

I suddenly realised that I was now involved in the very thing I had warned about: lowering a coffin with nothing to stop the ropes slipping out sideways. Mum was lowering on the other side of the grave and sure enough, about half way down, the coffin lurched sideways as the rope slipped out, the coffin lid came off and the dead dog, curled up as if asleep (and stiff with rigor mortis) burst out and became wedged against the side of the grave.

I still feel the horror across the many years. I got down onto my knees and flung my upper body into the grave, grabbing the edge of the cold dead animal and struggling to restore it to the coffin.

Above I could hear my mother saying, with the profoundest

of sincerity "I'm *so* sorry — this has never happened before". As I struggled I found some place for resentment that the very thing I had warned about was not just happening, it was happening to me.

Having a pet cemetery meant that we had to have a deep freezer for all the pet corpses that were awaiting burial. Inevitably people were constantly opening the wrong freezer when looking for things for the café, and coming across the grizzly sight of someone's beloved terrier, frozen solid.

Celia in the pet cemetery (photo: Elizabeth Kirkor Rogers)

Perhaps no story quite sums up the combination of extreme stress and absurdity of running a pet cemetery at Badsell as that told by Mum's dearest of friends, Elizabeth Kirkor Rogers.

It was some time in the early 1990s when Lizzie flew across from New York for a visit. She landed at Gatwick Airport and

CHAPTER 20

Mum picked her up in a little white Peugeot 504 belonging to her mother, Ruth.

In the front of the car with Mum was her Jack Russell, Lady, and, as she explained to Lizzie, in the boot of the car was another dog — this one dead and frozen, lying as though asleep in a large plastic dog bed.

Why had Mum seen fit to take a dead dog on a trip to Gatwick airport? She explained that the animal's funeral was scheduled for later and she did not want the mourners, who were coming down from London, to have to pet a rock hard frozen dog.

Now the obvious point — that the dog would have defrosted just as effectively without being taken on a round-trip ride to Gatwick - was not made at the time by Lizzie. She simply accepted that this was just business as usual at Badsell. Mum's logic, however, was probably sound. There wasn't really anywhere at Badsell where you could safely defrost a dog without some mischief befalling it.

After collecting Lizzie from the airport, Mum drove back to Kent but instead of going straight to the farm they went first to Matfield to the Post Office and Cherry Trees Tea Gallery, intending to visit Betty Waggitt and possibly have some lunch with her. Although her husband Bill was in, Betty was out so they drove to the car park of The Star for a couple of prawn salads. Mum had her usual white wine and Lizzie went for what she calls an 'English hard cider'.

After they paid they went out into the parking area to find that the car was no longer there. It had vanished with the live dog in the front and the dead dog in the boot.

They rushed back into the pub, then walked next door to Mark the butcher, who Mum knew well. Mark called the police.

They were of course absolutely frantic - the burial was due

to take place in an hour and of course Mum absolutely adored Lady, as she did all her Jack Russells.

It was a horrific situation.

Celia and Elizabeth Kirkor Rogers in The Star
before panic set in

At this point they decided to go back to the Cherry Trees Tea Gallery to see if Betty Waggit was there.

They left the butcher's shop and walked dejectedly towards The Cherry Trees Tea Gallery, hoping Betty had returned and would commiserate with them. As they approached, lo and behold, parked right in front stood the little white car with Lady sticking her head out the window, yapping with joy that they had finally remembered her. They hadn't driven to the pub and parked, they had just walked over the road.

It had all been hysteria over absolutely nothing.

They still had time to get ready for the funeral, the hole was already dug and the nice couple from London were able to pet and even kiss a dog that was at ambient temperature, unaware of the dramas that had occurred minutes before.

During the funeral there was another near-incident, possibly because Mum and Lizzie's nerves were now frazzled.

The owners threw a few of the dog's favourite toys and other mementos into the grave, before throwing a few symbolic handfuls of earth onto the coffin. One object that was tossed in was a big round, stainless steel water bowl.

It happens that Mum had mentioned to Lizzie that she needed to get a new water bowl for Lady because hers was cracked. As the bowl was being thrown into the grave, Mum and Lizzie's eyes met and they both had the same thought: 'just what we need!'

This reading of minds, the wicked idea that they might retrieve the bowl, the recent stress and drama, all contributed to a bout of near giggling. Luckily they got a hold of themselves quickly and I can report that the bowl was dutifully buried along with everything else. In fact you could argue that this entire story is something of an anti climax but I think it is illustrative of how, at Badsell, things always seemed to work out, even though we were often teetering on the edge of chaos.

AFTERWORD

I no more want to go into the story of how Badsell was sold than I would wish to describe my mothers final illness and passing.

Suffice it to say that one day the overdraft grew too large for the manager at Lloyds Bank, Tonbridge branch, and Badsell had to be sold quickly. Determined that as many staff as possible should keep their jobs and that the animals would not all be sold off, my parents searched for a buyer who would continue to run the petting zoo. It reduced the value considerably, but it was the honourable thing to do.

Badsell Park Farm will never be just land and buildings to me. It is really a family member who I love very much. When a person dies you can never see them again, but Badsell is close to where I live today and I still visit.

The buildings are now mostly homes and the land is owned by different people, but I am lucky enough to know several of them. Thanks to Adam Wise, who owns the land, I have been camping more than once with my children at the top of the sloping field and, thanks to John and Sandy Schofield, we have fished at the pond down the drive. James and Kate Cooper, who now own the farmhouse, have been kind enough to let me take my children to play in the maze which I designed more than thirty years ago and is now a mature and fabulous feature (and a huge pain to clip - sorry James!).

Each time I have been back it has got a little easier. I have got to the point where I can enjoy the beauty of the place without feeling a sense of loss.

On one occasion, when John and Sandy lived in the farmhouse, I visited an art exhibition in the big drawing room - but it was a step too far. As I walked towards the front door porch I started to have the sense that I was being flung back in time. Would Minnie, the Jack Russell, charge down the corridor, crash against the front door, then greet me on the porch, her whole body wagging? Maybe I would glimpse Mum in the kitchen through the open door at the far end? I turned right into the big drawing room and walked around the exhibition, but I couldn't see anything and I left quickly.

We lived at Badsell Park Farm from 1966 to 1996. The farm - the land it is on - existed for thousands of years before we lived there and it will exist for thousands of years into the future.

To all future custodians of Badsell Park Farm - please let nature thrive there.

It is a special place.

MY FRIEND CELIA BY ELIZABETH KIRKOR ROGERS

Celia and I met at age eight in 1946 at Channing School, Highgate, in North London. She had arrived from India the previous year and I had just arrived from New York City where I had spent the War years, so we were both a bit unusual. When I arrived at the school, I was suddenly aware of how different I was from the other girls; e.g. "Pass the word, the new girl's family drinks milk that's gone bad." (There was no yoghurt yet in England). Then, "Pass the word, the new girl does not wear knickers!" (because I would not take off my brown tunic for gym since I only wore brief, white, American underpants.) There were other humiliations, but Celia, bless her, was intrigued by the Kirkor family's oddities and, having a curious nature, just enjoyed them. So maybe that and her having lived in India for her first five years and being different in her own way, drew us together initially.

She was very imaginative and slightly disobedient which I loved because I was a bit of a goody-goody. One of our punishments was having to go to school on Saturday and sit in silence for an hour. I was subjected to this only once, Celia a bit more often!

When we were still at Channing School, my mother invited Celia and her mother Ruth to 1 Cranley Gardens in Muswell Hill, where we lived in north London. It was a lovely sunny day and in the garden Celia and I put on a scene from Alice in Wonderland. Celia played the Caterpillar, sitting on a large mushroom smoking a hookah, and I played Alice. Our audience consisted of the two mothers who, of course, thought the scene was splendid!

After several years the Thornely family moved to Goudhurst, a quaint little village in Kent, and I would often be invited to spend a month or so with them. I loved being there. Celia and I shared a bedroom and at night we would tiptoe to the window and listen to the bawdy songs being sung by the Cockney hoppickers at the Chequers pub down the road, the women often prancing around on the tables. We once joined the hop pickers at work and tossed hops into a long canvas sling while a horse pulled a cart around the periphery of the hop garden, collecting the hops.

I remember Celia borrowing a large, piebald, neighbour's horse and sharing it with me. She would ride the horse and I would ride a bicycle, then we would switch. The patient horse did not seem to mind the glass bottle with lemonade slung from his neck as well as the pack of sandwiches fixed for us by Celia's lovely mother, Ruth. There were other horses we borrowed as well and we would sometimes linger by a blacksmith at work at his anvil. The Kent countryside had so much of interest in the old days and the two of us had such enviable freedom to roam.

After Celia and Simon got married, they bought Badsell Park Farm and, again, I would be invited to spend lots of time enjoying it and helping out. I remember aiding Celia to shampoo a huge Gloucester Old Spot sow because it had some skin condition. I also assisted at the birth of a few lambs and learned to milk a goat. One summer, I had barely arrived from New York, when Celia plonked me down in the kitchen and told me to pluck some pheasants. There is a first and a last time for everything. At Badsell there was always something that needed doing, fixing, mending, or building. Animals that had to be fed, captured, shoed or dunked in disinfectant.

I did try to help Celia on the farm by tidying things up. Ruth said: "Lizzie, you'll never get Celia to be tidy", But I kept trying! I remember putting plastic stacking shelves next to the fridge with all the Preston's names on them. That worked for a week or so! My memory of the large kitchen table was of sundry papers and letters at one end, a brace of unplucked pheasants at the other, and a cheesecloth full of clotted milk (I think) hanging from the overhead lamp, dripping into a bowl - and a variety of other edibles and non-edibles scattered throughout. However Celia was so creative that maybe it was just as well that she did not waste her energies on tidiness but put it all into creativity. I also remember how it did not matter how many uninvited guests arrived at lunch or dinnertime, Celia always managing to feed them. Talk about the Miracle of the Loaves and Fishes!

Ernie Wiseman with John and Roland Rogers. John wearing Frank Thornely's helmet from the First World War (Photo: Elizabeth Kirkor Rogers)

The first time I saw Badsell, the farm was mainly producing corn. This was before the Government paid Celia and Simon **not** to plant corn due to a glut. As an animal lover, I was delighted by all the animals that later appeared. Celia asked me to help take care, appropriately enough, of the Polish hen and rooster – they were white, if I remember correctly, and had unusually fuzzy legs. I had to round them up at night into a long, wire-covered pen to flummox the fox.

My sons all adored Badsell. John loved driving the tractor and Roland was singled out to catch the escaped llama. Andy once shot a certain fox which endeared him to Celia who did not approve of the fox viewing her well-loved chickens as dinner! I often helped out selling produce in the farm's grocery shop. Celia was amused that a "university graduate" had trouble figuring out the newly-introduced pennies and pounds.

I remember that Celia had a contract with British Airways to provide them with strawberries. We once drove together to Heathrow to deliver them very early in the morning. Another time Celia was asked by a local farmer if she could rent out her male goat to impregnate his female. We put the goat in the back of the car and I was amused to see the most lascivious expression on an animal that I have ever encountered. He must have enjoyed his assignment and the farmer told us later that it bore fruit! Or rather, a kid!

Celia and I found the same things funny, loved animals and, our mothers got along beautifully. Ruth was always very warm and welcoming to me, except when she corrected my American English, e.g. "Lizzie, it is twenty to two not 'twenty of two,'" and, "Lizzie, do not say 'gotten.'" I found out, decades later, that Shakespeare used "gotten." I wish I had known it at the time. But when Celia and I were painting the family bicycles when the Thornelys lived in Goudhurst, I found the strange long wires on Ruth's bicycle getting in the way of my paint job, so I cut them off. They turned out to be her gear wires! But Ruth did not reprimand me at all. As for Frank Thornely, I did so enjoy him. After one of Ruth's lovely meals, he would get us kids into the kitchen and line us up to do the drying while he did the washing up. He used the time to tell us stories and regale us with jokes I wonder if modern dishwashing machines elicit such happy memories!

I loved going around Badsell, taking photographs, but, once in a while, I would sketch something. One day, I remember going into The Old Orchard where there was a flock of sheep called Soay. They were darkish in colour and quite skittish. Near them there was a large horse, maybe the one belonging to the gypsies. They were either uninterested or scared of me and kept their distance. So, I just sat down and began to draw. After a few minutes I became aware of feeling surrounded. I looked up and, lo and behold, the horse and some of the sheep had made a circle around me and were looking over my shoulder to see what I was up to! A very strange but welcome feeling.

Our families got on so well. Celia was very fond of my mother and brother, Andy, and she wrote me such sweet letters when they died. When my father died she wrote to my mother in a letter dated January 1983, "We have known each other so long that the sadness I feel at Stash's death encompasses all the years starting with the Caterpillar play from "Alice in Wonderland" through all the years: Goudhurst, my Father's death, Andy. Happy and sad times. All the time a close friendship even if there were long gaps."

Whenever I flew from the U.S. to England, I always especially looked forward to staying at Badsell, enjoying all the Prestons and Ruth Thornely and helping out with the animals. Celia always was so welcoming to my three boys and they, in turn, loved being "on the farm." I am grateful to Celia for her loving and steadfast friendship and I am delighted that our kiddies are taking that friendship into the fourth generation!

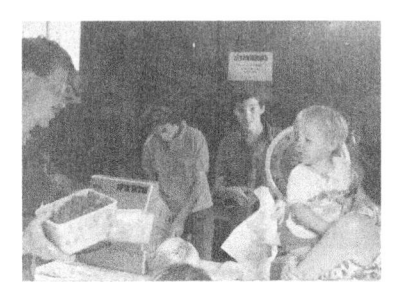

Andy Rogers serving PYO customers in the farm shop with Olivia, a girl who stayed on the farm to learn English (circa 1987)

Celia meant so much to me. She was my very oldest friend in England, we always had such fun together and often had each other in stitches of laughter. I loved her sense of adventure and exploration. I admired her horsemanship and courage and her culinary talents, I being nowhere near her equal in those departments. She was also an original and talented artist (my own artistic abilities developed much later when I started painting Manhattan streets scenes).

I wanted Adam to write this book because Celia and her family are such a big part of my life. We have shared so many of Life's happenings, both happy and sad, and I think the Preston and Thornely's lives, works and values represent the best that England has to offer. England welcomed us when my father refused to have us return to a Poland that had had Communism forced down its throat. Britain acknowledged the important participation of many Polish pilots in the Battle of Britain and of her military in other areas of conflict and therefore many Poles remained in Britain. It was hard to adjust at first but, with the help of Celia's family, we had a good life in England.

Also, I have read the James Herriot books that paid such colourful homage to the English countryside and I thought someone should immortalise Badsell so others could partake in the fun!

Celia and Elizabeth on the farmhouse terrace

MY SISTER, CELIA, BY NICK THORNELY

Celia was my younger sister, but in our teens, she looked 3 years older than me and everyone thought I was her younger brother, and I've always felt like the younger brother.

Celia was a gentle and lovely person but always up for an adventure. One of the first was riding pillion on my motor bike, a BSA 125 Bantam two stroke, when she was only 17. We toured France, Switzerland and Italy, staying at Youth Hostels, and whilst in Italy we saw the Italian girls riding side saddle on their scooters. She did the same. Alas, I crashed the bike and as she was wearing shorts, she burned her legs, We eventually had to get the burns treated in hospital.

When she was in Arizona with her friend Paulette, working at a Dude Ranch, she signed up for a Beauty Contest, and was crowned Miss Golden Nugget. She then entered a Steer Roping Contest at the local Rodeo and won that too. Her only reward was being shot in the backside by a drunk cowboy, and some of the pellets stayed in her bottom all her life. In fact they were picked up by an X Ray at Pembury Hospital.

She liked to travel and went to the Kentucky Derby with Carolyn, and later to Czechoslovakia to see the Pardubice steeplechase which is a race like the Grand National but much more dangerous.

In London, she shared a flat with Carolyn and Paulette and formed a lifelong friendship. She and Paulette were debutantes in 1956 and were in fact the second to last group to be formally presented to the Queen. Carolyn and her family are here today, as also is Paulette with her two daughters, which Celia and I called our Italian daughters. Celia and Simon 'adopted' Elena, and Ann and I 'adopted' Ciara.

Celia had many talents. Artist, dressmaker, cook and gardener. For her wedding in 1962 to Simon, she designed and made her own wedding dress and also the dresses for the 5 bridesmaids. Brother Anthony gave her away

Celia's presentation to Queen Elizabeth II as it appeared in a newspaper

Celia was a loving person and loved all animals and many were on view at Badsell Park Farm. She even loved pigs. And Mice! She found a family of mice nesting in her Range Rover, and instead of kicking them out, she left the door open so that they had easy entrance and exit.

Celia adored dogs and always worried about them. 'Where's Snippet?' was a constant query. She worried about the stray dogs in India and where they slept and who fed them. She loved the cows in India too, roaming round the beach and roads. She worried because she cared.

Celia loved all animals but above all dogs. She even loved Dead Dogs, and created The Orchard Pet Cemetery at Badsell Park Farm. Her brother Anthony's dog Beeney is buried at her home, Bohemia, but some of Anthony's ashes are actually buried in the Pet Cemetery at Badsell Park Farm.

One of Celia's greatest adventures was answering a BBC Advertisement to become a Landscape Gardener when she was 68 years old. There were over 4,000 applicants for 8 places. At the final selection the presenter Diarmuid Gavin said to the BBC Producer, "You do the final selection, but I must have Celia on my programme". Thus she took part in BBC 2 Garden School series, and insisted on wearing a hat for all the filming which was very stylish. She went on to design a Show Garden at BBC Gardeners' World Exhibition and won a Silver Medal for 'The Cereal Garden', doing all the planning and planting herself.

She also painted the 15 foot mural in the Conservatory at Bohemia. It is a picture of the Dahl Lake in Kashmir where the Thornely family spent two holidays in 1942 and 1943. The figure on the right, wearing a toper is our Dad, and the dachshund in the centre is called Jemima.

Dinner parties at Bohemia are my special memories. Celia would do the cooking in the Bohemia kitchen, which is more like an obstacle course than a kitchen, and would produce delicious meals for 6 to 16 people. She would still have time before dinner to drink Gin and Tonic and nibble cashew nuts, and then served huge platters of curry and rice. Simon sat at the far end of the table in the conservatory and lead the conversation with wit and there was always much laughter.

Above all, Celia was a matriarch and loved people of all ages. She was mother to five and grandmother to 10. She always had time to talk, always wanted to help and was always smiling. She was a very special person.

We are all <u>blessed</u> that she was a part of our lives.

Based on Nick Thornely's speech given at a celebration of her life at Bohemia, near Front, on the 14th May 2022

Celia with her 9th grandchild, Tabitha Belle Celia Preston, on the 27th September 2012

Celia Preston's funeral cortège pauses in Eridge Park, 5th January 2022

SIMON PRESTON

On the 5th August 2023 Simon Preston's 90th birthday was celebrated at Bohemia, near Frant. The following is based on a speech given by the author:

What a great joy and a privilege it is to be able to say that my father is still here to tell me to get my hair cut.

I am not going to attempt to tell Dad's life story, he has been in more scrapes than a flat bottomed boat, many of them actually in flat bottomed boats.

But a couple of things are worth saying on this momentous occasion.

The word 'unique' is over used but Dad is genuinely unique in that he is the only living person ever to have been publicly acknowledged as having worked undercover for SIS, the precursors of the British Secret Service now called MI6. In 1995 the Imperial War Museum put on an exhibition titled The Secret War, which included a series of exhibits telling how Dad worked undercover in the Austrian Alps, helping prepare for an expected Russian invasion of Western Europe . The exhibition ran for over twenty years.

Feeling that he could probably now tell his story, Dad began work on his autobiography. He informed MI6 that he was doing this and they called him in for a little chat.

'Preston' said an MI6 man ' we can't have you writing your memoirs.'

Dad then made the valid point that it was no longer a secret that he had been an MI6 operative, it was on display for all to see in a national museum - ' the cat is out of the bag,' he said.

The suave steely-eyed MI6 operative leaned forward, 'We want the cat put back in the bag.' He replied. Thus proving that despite the smoothness of the day-to-day running of MI6, they really don't understand the meaning of the 'cat out of the bag' metaphor. But being an honourable and loyal man, Dad shelved the autobiography,

In 1956 He assisted Hungarian Refugees pouring into Austria following the Soviet clamp down on their freedoms, helping in the establishment of a substantial refugee camp at Gussing. When Rupert, John, Charles and myself recently visited Gussing with Dad, over half a century after these events, he was treated as a celebrity and the local mayor treated us all to a slap up lunch.

In 1957 Dad was the first person, with two university friends, to be granted a tourist VISA into the USSR since the First World War. He drove across Western Europe and the entire USSR, by far the largest political entity in the world, in a Morris Minor with two friends, followed all the way by a huge Russian secret service vehicle full of people who, had they known that Dad had just been working against them for MI6 and had helped refugees escaping from Hungary, would have killed him.

Now of course there is a theme here which is that Dad clearly felt that it was important to keep a close eye on the Ruskies. He has never held enmity towards your individual

Rusky, but as a nation, they need to be watched. And I think we can now agree, with the invasion of Ukraine, that he was right all along.

Going back a bit I thought it was worth illustrating the enormous societal changes that Dad has lived through. He grew up in a harder world and his schooling was often harsh and brutal.

At the age of 5 he was sent to boarding school in Winchester before moving to a Prep school called Furzey Close. There two bullies, named Shannon and Engler, ran a reign of terror modelled on the Gestapo. Dad endured their favourite torture which involved throwing smaller boys, first stripped to the waist, off a twenty foot wall into a thicket of nettles. Incidentally the school closed down because it ran out of boys.

At Copthorne a boy called Goshen brought a revolver into school in a history class. He was dismantling it beneath his desk lid when it went off, sending a bullet clean through Goshen's hand. The history teacher, Mr Wier, who had survived everything the First World War could throw at him, died of shock shortly afterwards.

Despite all this the education Dad received was excellent and he was soon reciting Ciceros speeches in Latin. By the age of 11 he could chat easily in ancient Greek. Not particularly useful you might think but years later, while sailing through the Greek Islands, he was able to ask an old man tending some chickens, in a language not heard in those parts for three thousand years, if he could purchase his eggs. It's true that the word for eggs had evolved in that time, but the point is that when Dad asked that old man if he could purchase his testicles, the misunderstanding was the old man's fault for not attending an English prep school in the 1940's.

The ancient Greeks believed that the purpose of life was to undertake such deeds as to ensure you are immortalised in the stories told about you. We all have a treasure trove of stories about Dad's life but my birthday gift to Dad is a book titled Nato's Secret Armies, the Official History of the Secret Wars of the Modern Period. In the index you will find Preston (MI6 Agent) and the book recounts some of Dad's adventures, preserved for all time.

Dad you are much loved by your five children, your ten grandchildren and many other family and friends both gathered here and elsewhere. We all look forward to many happy years of your excellent company, and your wit and wisdom.

Dad's ten grandchildren then took it in turns to read from the following list of some of the roles he has played in his life:

1. Registered Cornish deep sea fisherman
2. Lieutenant, Royal Marine Commando
3. MI6 officer and spy, celebrated in the Imperial War Museum
4. Organiser of a refugee camp in Hungary
5. Van Driver for Selfridges
6. Crane Driver in London Docks
7. First Public Relations officer for the London Stock Exchange
8. Director or Chairman for a succession of Public Relations companies
9. Yachtsman (shipwrecked twice)
10. Entomologist
11. Farmer
12. Tourist Attraction Manager
13. Pet Cemetery Manager
14. Co-Director, Think British Campaign
15. Mentor to the Women's Farmer's Union
16. Snail Race Referee
17. Manager of Home for Retired Scarecrows.

ABOUT THE AUTHOR

Adam Preston is an artist, writer and film maker. He was born in 1966 and grew up at Badsell Park Farm in Kent. He has written for *The Times, The Financial Times, The Times Literary Supplement* and *Sight and Sound*. His novel *The Peppered Moth* describes a character, based on his father, who undergoes an unexpected transformation.

Adam's cartoons have appeared in *Private Eye* and one of his portraits hangs permanently in The Darwin House at Fitzwilliam College, Cambridge.

CONTACT

Please send any suggested corrections to adamprestonauthor@gmail.com

Badsell Park Farm has a Facebook page at https://www.facebook.com/badsellparkfarm

https://twitter.com/AdamPreston

Printed in Great Britain
by Amazon